Essays and Studies 1990

The English Association

The object of the English Association is to promote the knowledge and appreciation of English language and literature.

The Association pursues these aims by creating opportunities of co-operation among all those interested in English; by furthering the recognition of English as essential in education; by discussing methods of English teaching; by holding lectures, conferences, and other meetings; by publishing a journal, books, and leaflets; and by forming local branches overseas and at home.

Publications

The Year's Work in English Studies. An annual bibliography. Published by Basil Blackwell (USA.: Humanities Press).

Essays and Studies. An annual volume of essays by various scholars assembled by the collector, covering usually a wide range of subjects and authors from the medieval to the modern. Published by Basil Blackwell (USA: Humanities Press).

English. The journal of the Association, English, is published three times a year by the Association.

Newsletter. A Newsletter is published three times a year, giving information about forthcoming publications, conferences, and other matters of interest.

Benefits of Membership

Institutional Membership

Full members receive copies of The Year's Work in English Studies, Essays and Studies, English (3 issues) and three *Newsletters.*

Ordinary Membership covers *English* (3 issues) and three *Newsletters.*

Schools Membership includes two copies of each issue of *English,* one copy of *Essays and Studies,* three *Newsletters,* and preferential booking and rates for various conferences held by the Association.

Individual Membership

Individuals take out Basic Membership, which entitles them to buy all regular publications of the English Association at a discounted price, and attend Association gatherings.

For further details write to The Secretary, The English Association, The Vicarage, Priory Gardens, London W4 1TT.

Essays and Studies 1990

Fictional Space

Essays on Contemporary Science Fiction

Edited by
Tom Shippey

for the English Association

Basil Blackwell, Oxford
Humanities Press
Atlantic Highlands, NJ

ESSAYS AND STUDIES 1991
IS VOLUME FORTY-THREE IN THE NEW SERIES
OF ESSAYS AND STUDIES COLLECTED ON BEHALF OF
THE ENGLISH ASSOCIATION

First published 1991
by Basil Blackwell Ltd
108 Cowley Road, Oxford,
OX4 1JF

British Library Cataloguing in Publication Data

A CIP catalogue record for this book is available from the British Library.

First published 1991 in the United States of America by
HUMANITIES PRESS INTERNATIONAL. INC.,
Atlantic Highlands, NJ 07716

The Library of Congress has cataloged this serial
publication as follows:

Essays and studies (London England: 1950)
Essays and studies: being volume 43 of the new series of essays
and studies collected for the English Association.—1950-
—Oxford: Basil Blackwell Ltd, [1950-
v.:ill.:22cm.
AAT8342 Annual.

Title varies slightly
Vols. for 1950-1981 called also new ser..v.S.v.34.
Continues: English studies (London England)

1 English literature—History and criticism. 2 English philology—Collections. I. English Association. II. Title. III. Title: Essays & studies.
PR1$.E4 820.4 36-8431
AACR 2 MARC-S

Library of Congress [8509-85] rev 5
ISBN 0-631-17762-0 (Basil Blackwell)
ISBN 0-631-17763-9 (pbk) Basil Blackwell
for the English Association only
ISBN 0-391-03688-2 (Humanities Press)

Typeset by Setrite Typesetters Ltd., HK
Printed and bound in Great Britain by Billing and Sons Ltd,
Worcester

Contents

Note on References

Too many works of science fiction are mentioned in this volume for them all to be annotated. Accordingly, references are given in notes only to those works undergoing substantial discussion. In all other cases, date of first publication is given in the text, to enable readers to grasp relative chronology, while a full reference (subject to the caveat there printed) is given in the bibliography of works cited at the end. Historical and critical works are noted as usual, and also included in the bibliography.

Preface: Learning to Read Science Fiction

TOM SHIPPEY

None of the essays in this volume (including this one) spends very much time in discussing definitions of science fiction, or what science fiction is. There are good practical reasons for this: science fiction is not a new form in terms of most individuals' reading-experience, it is readily identifiable and regularly identified on a commercial basis by readers, publishers and bookshop-managers; it has in a sense defined itself. Nevertheless, another and more ignoble reason is that previous attempts to define it have proved so unsuccessful;[1] no one wants to venture into a critical quagmire.

Yet around this absence of precise or agreed definition circle questions of interest not only to pedants or lexicographers, but to general readers and to students of the entire field of contemporary writing. Is science fiction, for instance, a field which draws its importance and relevance from a covert or metaphorical referentiality to its own real present (as implied in quite different ways by Spark and Elms below)? Or – since the real present so quickly goes out of date, while we can see now that even our grandparents' science fiction does not always follow suit – does science fiction draw its value, or some of its value, from mere or utter 'futuristic play' (an idea brought up by Huntington, see p. 62 below)? Not entirely unconnected with the pair of questions above, does science fiction have or need a close relationship with the 'science' its generic title suggests as a defining feature; or can it continue as fiction after its 'science' has become outdated, or been revealed as pseudo-science, or after its computer-conscious author has been exposed as a man who never progressed beyond the typewriter and returned his first word-processor on the ground that when he switched it on, it just buzzed and flashed lights at him?[2] Not far away from these issues of novelty and relevance lie others: is science fiction an inherently conservative form in literary terms (as suggested below by Meyers and partly corroborated by Christie), or is it intrinsically radical, a trampler of taboos (as implied by Shippey and Spark)? Does it use an 'independent economy of signs' (see p. 38 below), or is it parasitic upon the greater body of literary fiction? Is it emerging from a 'ghetto', or wrapping exclusion luxuriously around its shoulders? Has it been strengthened or diluted by transition from the world of specialist magazines to instant popular-medium success via *Star Trek* or *Star Wars*? What is its relationship to fantasy fiction, is its readership still dominated by male adolescents, is it a taste which will ever appeal to the mature but non-eccentric literary mind?

Of all these questions, it is perhaps the last which gives most opportunity for a firm step forward towards definition. Many times in the past twenty years the present writer has been told, usually by academic colleagues of some sophistication, that they 'never read science fiction, just can't read science fiction, don't see how anyone gets anything out of science fiction'. The experience is too common for the statements not to be true. There are many people who simultaneously cannot bear science fiction and never read it; but though they cannot bear it they recognize it immediately. Nor is the repulsion they feel built up cumulatively over pages and chapters, or based selectively on dislike of particular plots, authors, styles, etc. It is *instant* and *universal*. It is, in fact, a generic reaction, and there is accordingly at least a chance of defining the field of science fiction, so to speak, by ricochet; its detractors may not know much about the genre, but they do know what they don't like. What triggers this reaction?

The inner nature of science fiction may be exposed by comparing two passages, very similar in content and style, but one inside the field and one outside it. The 'outsider' is the start of George Orwell's novel of 1939, *Coming up for Air*:[3]

> The idea really came to me the day I got my new false teeth.

I remember the morning well. At about a quarter to eight I'd nipped out of bed and got into the bathroom just in time to shut the kids out. It was a beastly January morning, with a dirty yellowish-grey sky. Down below, out of the little square of bathroom window, I could see the ten yards by five of grass, with a privet hedge round it and a bare patch in the middle, that we call the back garden. There's the same back garden, same privets, and same grass, behind every house in Ellesmere Road. Only difference – where there are no kids there's no bare patch in the middle.

I was trying to shave with a bluntish razor-blade while the water ran into the bath. My face looked back at me out of the mirror, and underneath, in a tumbler of water on the little shelf over the washbasin, the teeth that belonged in the face. It was the temporary set that Warner, my dentist, had given me to wear while the new ones were being made. I haven't such a bad face, really. It's one of those bricky-red faces that go with butter-coloured hair and pale-blue eyes. I've never gone grey or bald, thank God, and when I've got my teeth in I probably don't look my age, which is forty-five.

Quite how many things Orwell is trying to say in this passage is arguable. But probably from the 250 words cited one could easily make a list of some twenty to twenty-five data – a *datum* being a discrete fact stated or implied in the passage, such as: 'the narrator's house has a bathroom', or 'the narrator's house has a garden', or 'the narrator's house has only one bathroom', or 'the narrator has children' (with whom, inferentially, he has to share the bathroom), etc. In addition to these, we could easily generate a string of more debatable conclusions, such as 'the narrator tries to economize on razor-blades, even though these are/were cheap', or 'the inhabitants of Ellesmere Road include retired or unmarried people, who have no children'. A fuzz of such speculation must in some way surround the reading experiences of this passage; but sensible readers will not take it too far, for they may know, e.g., that Orwell was particularly irritated by blunt razor-blades, or may suspect that the demographic make-up of Ellesmere Road does not need to be imagined too precisely for the purpose of the fiction.

Yet what most readers work out from their twenty to twenty-five data must be something like this:

1 The narrator (to use Northrop Frye's 'theory of literary modes') is 'low mimetic', and on the verge of becoming ironic. He has false teeth, a sign of age, but also in 1930s England a strong sign of non-upper social class;[4] he is middle-aged, his appearance is undistinguished, we will learn in the next paragraph that he is fat.

2 The narrator is clearly 'middle-class', or what would now be categorized as 'C1': his house has

only one bathroom, the w.c. is in it, there are at least four people to share it (counting the children's inferential mother). Mornings are accordingly competitive occasions when it comes to using the bathroom. But this major inconvenience is dictated by economy, as is the size of the garden, and the bare patch in it which tells us that children play in their gardens (sc. because they have nowhere else to go). Orwell is particularly clear about these class-marking details: the narrator is a house-*owner*, and the house has a garden (so it is not a 'back-to-back', a working-class house). But it is a small garden directly under the bathroom window, and the window itself is a 'little' one. On the information already given, most English readers, in 1939 *or* 1989, could and would make accurate guesses about the narrator's income and life-style. That is what Orwell wants them to do.

3 The narrator's life-style is a drab one. Whether this fact should be related to his class status, whether drabness is a necessary part of 'low mimesis', these are precisely the themes of the novel (which says in short that they are all related but, very passionately, ought not to be). Just the same, the fact is there, in the 'beastly' morning, the 'dirty' sky, the 'little' square of window, the 'bare' patch of garden, the 'bluntish' razor-blade, and so on: of the twenty-five adjectives in the passage, nine are clearly derogatory, others ('same' and 'only') inferentially so, yet others ('bad', 'grey', 'bald') sug-

gestive above all of the narrator trying to cheer himself up. Stylistically, the main qualities one might identify in the passage are its directness and single-mindedness. Orwell, it seems, has only a few things to say; while he will substantiate these with many details, all the details will point in one direction.

It is this which makes *Coming Up for Air* such a satisfactory if elementary example of how a non-science-fiction novel works. There is no doubt about its data; very little about what the data mean; and though there are some details of whose meaning a non-native or non-contemporary reader might be doubtful, like the privet hedge or the 'quarter to eight' rising,[5] they cause no serious trouble because they confirm or are confirmed by all the others. In the whole passage there is no jarring or inconsistent note.

Compare a matching passage from science fiction, again the opening of a novel, again a man shaving: this time from Frederik Pohl and C. M. Kornbluth's novel of 1953, *The Space Merchants*:[6]

> As I dressed that morning I ran over in my mind the long list of statistics, evasions, and exaggerations that they would expect in my report. My section – Production – had been plagued with a long series of illnesses and resignations, and you can't get work done without people to do it. But the Board wasn't likely to take that as an excuse.
>
> I rubbed depilatory soap over my face and rinsed it

with the trickle from the fresh-water tap. Wasteful, of course, but I pay taxes and salt water always leaves my face itchy. Before the last of the greasy stubble was quite washed away the trickle stopped and didn't start again. I swore a little and finished rinsing with salt. It had been happening lately; some people blamed Consic saboteurs. Loyalty raids were being held throughout the New York Water Supply Corporation; so far they hadn't done any good.

The morning newscast above the shaving mirror caught me for a moment ... the President's speech of last night, a brief glimpse of the Venus rocket squat and silvery on the Arizona sand, rioting in Panama. . . I switched it off when the quarter-hour time signal chimed over the audio band.

It looked as though I was going to be late again. Which certainly would not help mollify the Board.

I saved five minutes by wearing yesterday's shirt instead of studding a clean one and by leaving my breakfast juice to grow warm and sticky on the table. But I lost the five minutes again by trying to call Kathy. She didn't answer the phone and I was late getting into the office.

How long is it, one might ask, before a reader who does not already know realizes that this *is* science fiction? And how does such a reader realize? The answer must be (a) on reading 'depilatory soap' and (b) on realizing in rapid succession that depilatory soap does not exist, that for it to exist some sort of chemical breakthrough would be necessary, that such a breakthrough nevertheless would be exploited, just like freeze-dried coffee. The reader of this phrase is in fact – if male and middle-aged – likely to remember a string of shaving-technology innovations, from the aerosol can of shaving cream to the coated blade to the double blade, with the concomitant development of electric, cordless and rechargeable-battery razors; and at once to note the fact of a progression, to set 'depilatory soap' in that progression, to realize it is as yet an imaginary stage, but also that the existence of such stages (all at one time imaginary) is by no means imaginary. 'Depilatory soap' is not-real; but it is not-unlike-real. That, in miniature, is the experience of reading science fiction. As well as recognizing data, you recognize non-data; but since these are data within the story, they are well labelled '*nova data*', 'new things given'. The basic building-block of science fiction (the term is Darko Suvin's) is accordingly the *novum*[7] – a discrete piece of information recognizable as not-true, but also as not-unlike-true, not-flatly- (and in the current state of knowledge) impossible.

How many novums, in the sense given, are there in the passage quoted? Probably, around fifteen. Some are easily identifiable: there is no more doubt about the depilatory soap than about Orwell's 'bare patch'. At the other extreme – as with Orwell's 'quarter to eight' – there are cases where a non-

American or non-contemporary may be unsure whether he or she is confronting a novum or a datum. The 'quarter-hour time signal...over the audio band' sounds futuristic, but then time signals on radio and TV are now common enough. And what is meant by 'wearing yesterday's shirt instead of studding a clean one'? All my shirts have buttons on. Are the authors talking about collar-studs (old technology), or maybe some future novelty, like paper disposable shirts, of which the only non-recycled bits are the studs that replace buttons? In both cases there may be uncertainty, in both cases (again as with Orwell) suspended till more information comes in.

There is after all a great deal of information in this passage, though the experienced science fiction reader is unlikely to hesitate over it. Water, for instance: salt water comes out of the tap (one novum); so does fresh, but it trickles; using fresh water for washing is 'wasteful, *of course*'; fresh water is supplied by the government to which the narrator pays taxes. There is a string of novums here, but no reader can register them without making some attempt to put them together. In this world, we realize, natural resources are unexpectedly scarce; so scarce that only government can be allowed to control them; this narrator is not entirely loyal to his government. There is a similar string of novums and inferences at the end of the second paragraph. 'It had been happening lately' implies (a) change, (b) recent change, (c) frequent occurrence, so, potentially irreversible change. 'So far they hadn't done any good' backs up the notion of irreversibility. More inferences come, however, from the five words 'some people blamed Consie saboteurs'. 'Some people' implies 'not everyone' and in particular not the narrator. 'Consie' even now – and still more in 1953 – sets up the parallel with 'Commie'. If 'Commie' ‹ 'Communist', what is the missing term in the sequence 'Consie' ‹ ...? An astute reader might guess the answer 'Conservationist' (by inference from the interest in fresh water). But any 1953 reader was likely to note:

1. in this world, Communists are no longer a threat. But,
2. McCarthyite attitudes are still present. So,
3. if 'Commies' were just a scapegoat, maybe 'Consies' are too. This is backed up by the failure of the 'loyalty raids', as point 2 is by their existence.

But this last inference, when contrasted with those stemming from the fresh water/salt water opposition, raises a further query more basic to the structure of the whole novel. If 'Consies' cannot be blamed for the potentially irreversible change coming over the narrator's horizon, what can? Something, clearly, which neither the government nor the sceptical narrator would like to think about:

it is, to be brief, the ghost of Thomas Malthus in horrible alliance with the descendants of the Coca Cola Company. Limited resources are bad enough. When they coexist with an ethic which demands continuous increases in consumption (and does not scruple to use physical and emotional addiction to get these increases), then you have the ground rules for the Pohl and Kornbluth 'dystopia'.

But it does not start with ground rules. It starts with novums. To read *The Space Merchants* – to read any science fiction – one has first to recognize its novums, and then to *evaluate* them. There is a discernible and distinguishable pleasure at each stage, as you realize how things are different, how they are similar, and go on to wonder, and to discover, what causes could have produced the changes, as also – and this is a 'referentiality' from which science fiction can never entirely escape – to speculate what causes have produced the effects of the real world, the effects with which we are so familiar that in most cases they are never given a thought. It is true that readers are unlikely to stop and chew over the implications of 'depilatory soap' or 'Consie saboteurs' in the way that this discussion has done, but then readers of Orwell do not stop to boggle over the implications of 'bare patch in the middle' or 'get into the bathroom just in time' either. Yet the latter group certainly understands at some level that Orwell is writing about class. The reader of *The Space Merchants* likewise soon has a clear idea that its authors are attacking the American way of life, or consumer-culture.

But it is not that message (I suspect) which would have made *The Space Merchants* literally unreadable to the many literate and liberal colleagues who have voiced distaste for science fiction over the years. It is the existence in science fiction of the novum, and of the pattern of intellectual inference to be drawn from it. Darko Suvin's definition of science fiction, indeed, is that it is:

> a literary genre whose necessary and sufficient conditions are the presence and interaction of estrangement and cognition, and whose main formal device is an imaginative framework alternative to the author's empirical environment.[8]

'Estrangement', with reference to the examples given, means recognizing the novum; 'cognition' means evaluating it, trying to make sense of it. You need both to read science fiction. Some people are willing to do neither.

What causes this reluctance may well be beyond the scope of literary criticism; it could be, for instance, that those deeply and personally attached to the status quo will refuse even the notion that reality is an accident, the result of the interaction of a host of social and technical variables, any of which might have been different and all of which are still varying. One might note here the remarks of John

Huntington below (pp. 62–4) about 'habitus' and class feeling. Huntington suggests that the truly revolutionary element of Wells's *Time Machine* in 1895 was not the 'scientific gesture' of the time machine itself, but the 'significant shifts in class allegiances' signalled by the Eloi and the Morlocks, a shift perhaps repeated – Huntington further suggests – in the 'hacker vs. corporation' world of William Gibson's *Neuromancer* nearly ninety years later. Huntington feels that these suggestions rather qualify Suvin's thesis of 'cognitive estrangement', which he thinks gives too much dignity to 'conscious rationality' as opposed tacitly to class (or other) prejudice. But, as has been said above, this depends on what one means by 'cognition'. The reader of *The Space Merchants* may not brood over Consies/Commies and may very well not detect Pohl and Kornbluth's real-life and by American standards distinctly left-wing political stance.[9] Nevertheless one cannot read science fiction at all without *some* recognitions and *some* evaluations: quite how 'cognitive' these low-level cognitions or recognitions may be does not seem too vital. What one could say – see Shippey and Spark below, *passim* – is that science fiction does provide a consistent medium by which writers can consider political issues, like Vietnam or threats to American hegemony, without accepting the battle-lines of contemporary politics. In this sense science fiction is often a continuing adventure in new 'structures of feeling'. And, to resolve an opposition set up at the start of this essay, it can be both 'referential' and 'playful' at once, and not necessarily most referential when least playful (see 'The New Atlantis', pp. 117–19 below) or vice versa ('Criticality', pp. 119–24).

There is a further conclusion one can come to by considering the basic actions of reading science fiction. It is that science fiction must intrinsically be a 'high-information' literature. 'Information', as the *Oxford English Dictionary* tells us, has in recent years become a technical as well as a colloquial term. It now means (see *OED Supplement*, vol. II, 1976):

> As a mathematically defined quantity ... now esp. one which represents the degree of choice exercised in the selection or formation of one particular symbol, sequence, message etc., out of a number of possible ones, and which is defined logarithmically in terms of the statistical probabilities of occurence of the symbol or the elements of the message.

This sense seems to have become common only after World War II, and to be associated with 'information theory' and cybernetics. There is a literary point to be drawn from it, though, and it is this. In English, as in other languages, there is a high degree of 'redundancy'. Some words can be readily predicted from their context, especially 'grammatical' as opposed to 'lexical' items. If, for instance, the fifth or the seventh word of the Orwell passage were to be blanked out, and the rest of the sentence left, few readers would have much trouble in filling them in. The same is true of the 'lexical' words 'came' or 'false' in that sentence. But by contrast, if 'nipped' in sentence three were to be blanked out, most readers would probably fill in, as first guess, 'got' or 'jumped' or 'climbed'. 'Nipped' is a higher-information word than 'came', or than 'the' in sentence one; it is less predictable, and there are more choices available to fill its slot. Just the same, few if any words in the Orwell passage are entirely unpredictable, or particularly surprising, distinctive though Orwell's style may be. The whole book is (no doubt deliberately) towards the low end of the English novel's generally 'medium-information' span.

Science fiction, however, to repeat the point, is intrinsically a 'high-information' genre. Novums, just because they are novums, are very hard to predict. Some of the words in the Pohl and Kornbluth passage would take many guesses to arrive at if they had been blanked out: one might guess 'fresh-water' from the antithesis with 'salt water', and 'depilatory' (as opposed to 'perfumed' or 'carbolic' or 'coal-tar') *if* one worked out from context that the passage was about shaving – this is not so obvious once 'depilatory' and 'stubble' are removed – but 'studding', 'Consie', and both elements of 'loyalty raids' seem to be inherently unpredictable. Yet Pohl and Kornbluth here, like Orwell within the English novel as a whole, are towards the low end of their genre's information-range. A glance at the first 250 words of, say, Gibson's *Neuromancer*, discussed so often below, will show just how high a 'high-information' style can go while remaining readable: I would suggest that it contains at least a dozen words, not counting names, which could never be accurately recovered by any hypothetical editor of the future, working as it might be from a single surviving damaged or rat-gnawed exemplar.

The science fiction reader, of course, *likes* this feeling of unpredictability. It creates intense curiosity, as well as the pleasure of working out, in the long run, the logic underlying the author's decisions, vocabulary and invented world. It is a powerful stimulus to the exercise of 'cognition', of putting unknown data into some sort of mental holding tank, to see if and when they start to fit together, and what happens when they do. Yet this experience is in a sense a deeply 'anxious' one: Huntington again remarks on this with particular reference to *Neuromancer*, and says well that any reader of that book is likely to feel all the time that he or she has missed something, failed to grasp 'more than an edge of the whole reality', is in fact a poor or inattentive reader. But that particular case is only an extreme example of one of the characteristic marks of science fiction: unease, a feeling that rules may be altered, a required readiness to accept the novum, the sudden jolt of 'high information'.

Perhaps the most concentrated form in which such jolts may be delivered is the neologism. Paragraph three of *Neuromancer* contains the word 'joeboys', a word which as far as I can see (but then like everyone else I am not a perfect reader) is nowhere explained. More significant in Gibson's world are the words 'cyberspace' and 'ice', the former a neologism meaning the world one enters/will enter on plugging the brain into the worldwide computer network of the future, the 'electronic consensus-hallucination that facilitates the handling and exchange of massive quantities of data', the latter a concealed acronym for Intrusion Countermeasures Electronics, the constant warfare inside cyberspace of 'watchdog programs', 'military black ice' and 'icebreakers'. Strikingly, both words have passed since 1984 into general science-fictional use: they express concepts too good not to use. The same is true of Ursula Le Guin's 'ansible', see Meyers, p. 206 below, a word for an as yet uninvented gadget. More suggestively, the whole of Le Guin's 1969 novel *The Left Hand of Darkness* may be taken as a meditation on the word 'shifgrethor', which means at once 'shadow' and 'an alien sense of honour': why 'shadow' and 'honour' should be related concepts is one challenge to cognition, perhaps resolved in the novel's quasi-allegorical chapter 18, 'On the Ice'. 'Shifgrethor', however, is a neologism so closely tied to the world of its book that it has not been borrowed. Words which *have* been borrowed from science-fiction novels into everyday reality include, from Le Guin's *The Dispossessed* (1974), 'kleggitch' (boring work, as opposed to exciting work, but work which has to be done, like housework, but not sexually linked), or, from Philip K. Dick's *Do Androids Dream of Electric Sheep?* (1968), 'kipple':

> Kipple is useless objects, like junk mail or match folders after you use the last match or gum wrappers or yesterday's homeopape. When nobody's around, kipple reproduces itself. For instance, if you go to bed leaving any kipple around your apartment, when you wake up the next morning there's twice as much of it. It always gets more and more.

Another likely candidate for future lexicographers is Kim Robinson's self-explanatory 'mallsprawl', from *The Gold Coast* (1988).

Words like these hang as it were on the edge of everyday experience, recognized instantly as filling a gap, but also betraying the existence of the gap. Sometimes they make one wonder why such a gap should exist. Why, for instance, is there in English no neutral-sex third-person singular pronoun—all our other personal pronouns are neutral—sex-equivalent to 'one' but not including the speaker, not being impersonal? Its absence has already led this essay into at least one clumsy 'he or she', and drives other writers (see Christie, below) into other expedients. Yet the gap usually goes unnoticed, or is accepted as natural. In the last section of *The Years of the City* (1984), however, Frederik Pohl rounds off his picture of a developing American utopia with a world in which such a pronoun is regularly used: instead of 'he/him/his' or 'she/her/hers', one says consistently 'e/um/uz'. Just to rub the point in, among the characters' casual words of abuse are the neutral-sex neologisms 'prunt' and 'fugger'. If these words were blanked out of the text, they would not be guessed; indeed, in the case of 'e/um/uz', one imagines that strict control would have to be exerted over sub-editors to ensure they stayed in at all, and were not automatically replaced by their 'obvious' equivalents. So they are 'high-information' items in terms of unpredictability. But once introduced they also point a powerful if silent finger at the terms one has come to expect. They make us aware of the latent presuppositions, the unconsidered information about our own habits concealed within casual and normal speech. In this way Pohl's coinages perhaps exemplify the 'tri-valency', the multiple relations between real and fictional worlds, seen in science fiction by Samuel Delany (see Spark, p. 133 below). And in addition they do one other thing: they serve as a warning that science fiction has a rhetoric of its own, an 'economy of signs' (to use Christie's phrase from p. 38 below), a hierarchy of figures of which the neologism is only the lowest term. The distinctive feature of this unconsidered rhetoric is its ability to exploit contrast, between the real world and the fictional, the novum and the datum, the real gap and the science-fictional filling of it. The tropes, images and modes of this rhetoric, however, have still not been codified; in a sense, critics have not yet learnt to read them.

There would be quite enough material for the beginning of a *Rhetorica nova* in the last section of Pohl's 1984 book.[10] It is called 'Gwenanda and the Supremes', which sounds like a pop group. But in this case 'Supremes' is an ellipsis for 'Supreme Court Justices': the first postulate of Pohl's fiction is that in this future world judges are chosen by lot (like modern jurymembers), trained, given computer guidance, and then allowed to settle matters not by the arcane and deliberately professionalized structures of modern Anglo-American law, but by common sense alone – common sense being, says Gwenanda, 'what the Second American Revolution was all about, right?' This means that from the start Gwenanda and her colleagues can behave, and talk, like an unruly pop group, in a Supreme Court setting of considerable gravity.

The contrast sets up a sequence of assaults on the modern reader's unconsidered assumptions about legal and stylistic decorum. Faced with a client who has murdered her husband ('uz marry' in their

English), the Chief Justice allows twenty minutes for a plea in mitigation, cuts the defendant off dead on time, and says (p. 262): 'Right ... I'd call this a case for summary judgement if we ever saw one, and I'll start the ball rolling. Guilty. How say you, gang? 'How say you?' is formal legal English; 'gang' is intimate/colloquial. The contrast feels disrespectful, and even more so are the notions of a judge dispensing 'summary judgement', and attempting without concealment to lead his colleagues. Shocks of this nature keep on being delivered. Later on, a defendant is betrayed when his lawyer approaches the bench and says: 'Well, what e said, when we were talking about uz case, was e said it cost um plenty to fugger up the records at the freezatorium' (p. 325). 'I protest the unethical behaviour of this attorney!' cries the defendant. 'I want him disbarred.' But 'fuggering up the records' has led to a plague in the future, from the germs of the past carried by a frozen-then-thawed invalid; and the only reason the defendant is surprised by what the lawyer has done is that he too is from the past, is indeed a corrupt judge from the legal system of the present. One obvious point is that to him 'unethical' does not mean 'morally wrong', it means – and to our shame, this is a standard modern meaning – 'against the customs of a profession'. The speech of the future ('gang', 'fugger', 'what e said ... was e said') is marked for us as careless, lax, or ugly. But in this story the speech of the characters from our time, while careful, precise, and formal, is presented also as deeply dishonest, 'professionalized' in the worst sense, full of genuinely evil or 'unethical' presumptions. Who is in the right? Which is more important, offended decorum or neglected justice?

The rhetorical questions above are mirrored by one in the text, again spoken by an unsympathetic revivee from modern times: 'What kind of a world would it be if you let people do whatever they wanted?' And the answer obviously generated by the text is 'quite a nice one', remembering always the Thirty-first Amendment to the Constitution of the United States, 'Nobody has any right to dump on anybody else. This takes precedence over ever-thing else.' But change of register, semantic shift, and rhetorical questioning are only three of the devices continually used, and used with great variety by Pohl, to set up the repeated contrast between future and present, to rouse the reader's alarm over the unknown future (the 'e/uz' level), and then demand why such alarm should not be better felt about the present (the 'he/she' level). Neologisms used in 'Gwenanda', besides those already cited, include 'an' (a person, neither (m)an nor (wom)an), 'muddy' (a parent, a mummy/daddy), 'hemale' and 'shemale', and 'congressun': at least they all follow a clear logic. By contrast, words from the present used and greeted with incomprehension or derision by the future include 'feet' (as a unit of measurement), 'attorney', 'testify', 'witness', 'bench', 'statement', 'prejudicial', 'competent authority': all are tagged by Pohl with the same legalistic narrow-mindedness as 'unethical', or the ethnocentrism of 'feet'.

Pohl also makes considerable play with the way in which speech is presented. Early on, the reader's sympathies are led at least two ways by a passage which shifts unexpectedly between authorial narration and what one might recognize as 'coloured' interior monologue.[11] Samelweiss, the Chief Justice, has just left in the middle of the defendant's speech to go to the toilet – wearing, it should be said, his 'walk-around headphones', a characteristic technological novum combined with sociological provocation. But:

> In fairness to Samelweiss, it was true that nothing was being said that any sensible person would want to hear. The brute of a defendant had begged for twenty minutes to make a statement, and Samelweiss, the old fool, had let her have it. Probably just wanted time to go to the can. So the statement had gone on for six or seven minutes already. Bor-*ing*. All she did was complain about the myriad ways in which society had so warped and brutalized her that whatever she did wasn't really her *fault*. Now she was only up to the tyrannical first-grade teacher who had hung the label of thief on her –
>
> A loud beep interrupted her – one of the Tin

Twins. 'Hold on there a minute, sweet-meats. You did swipe the teacher's wallet, didn't you?'

The defendant paused, annoyed at the interruption. 'What? Well, sure. But I was only a child, your Honor.'

'And then you did, the way it says here in the charge, you did stab your marry to death, right?'

'Only because society made me an outlaw, Your Honor.'

'Right,' said the Twin, losing interest (p. 260).

Any experienced reader of fiction, not just science fiction, will realize straight away that 'sensible' here is tendentious. The language at the start is Gwenanda's: 'old fool', 'go to the can', 'brute of a defendant', all are part of her sceptical, aggressive, overstating personality, and they establish Gwenanda as a familiar 'unreliable narrator'. Her judgements accordingly should be unreliable, and we expect to be against her because of her bias. But not all that paragraph sounds like her interior monologue. 'Bor-*ing*' no doubt is, but what about 'society', 'warped and brutalized', 'tyrannical', 'hung the label on'? These do not sound like Gwenanda, but like the defendant filtered through Gwenanda. But if they are the defendant's words, she sounds unreliable too. As for the self-exculpatory whine of 'wasn't really her *fault*', it is hard to tell whether this is the defendant speaking (as in 'because society made me an outlaw' in direct speech just below), or Gwenanda mocking ('*fault*' is like 'Bor-*ing*' just above). In practice, the reader is likely to take the defendant as a 'stooge', a dummy set up to voice attitudes respectable enough in our time, with Gwenanda as the new voice, the voice of the fiction challenging us. Yet with one unreliable narrator reporting another, it is hard to say which way sympathy would go. There is more than one irony in the paragraph. As the passage moves on to ordinary authorial narration plus unmediated direct speech, matters become clearer, but even so there is a sequence of shocks. 'Sweet-meats' and 'swipe' are highly unjudicial language, and there is again an indecorous anacoluthon in 'you did, the way it says here in the charge, you did . . .' Perhaps even more surprising is the fact that it is not only a judge speaking, but a robot. After dozens of post-Asimovian tales about self-sacrificing, human-worshipping robots, it is a shock especially for a science fiction reader to come upon '"Right," said the Twin, *losing interest*.' The remark itself is familiar to anyone who speaks English; 'Right' does not mean 'I agree', but 'I heard what you said'. Just the same, the casual nature of this continues the presentation of Pohl's future world as, in our terms, careless, harsh and biased. Yet this must coexist with the vision of our world and our language as, in the terms of the fiction, evasive, irresponsible, and dishonest.

Pohl's story in fact depends heavily on the presence of 'corpsicles';[12] twentieth-century people who have been frozen and then revived, to find themselves as centres of anachronism in the future, their familiar phrases and beliefs becoming, as it were, nova to the whole greater imagined novum. The device allows Pohl to exploit amazement both ways. Gwenanda's whole world is full of amazement to us. But when our world is put to her and her colleagues, they react with giggles, gasps, 'incredulous snickers', or even – when the 'adversary system' of Anglo-American justice is explained in brutal paraphrase – 'silence, broken by a beep'. The assertion is always that fictional and factual worlds have parity, that 'uz marry' is really no stranger than 'a thousand feet', 'swipe' or 'gang' no more indecorous than 'plaintiff' or 'testify'. At the end of the process even common words are tinged with uncertainty. Like other writers, Pohl uses adverbs to indicate tone of voice – 'indignantly', 'reasonably' – or mental attitude. Yet what is one to make of the last words of the first scene (p. 268), as Gwenanda sentences the marry-stabber to indefinite freezing: '"You can take um away, Sam. And get um a nice dinner," she added kindly, "because it'll have to last um a long time."'

In normal fiction, 'kindly' would be bitterly ironic; it would show Gwenanda as a latter-day Judge Jeffreys, exulting in her own power and her victim's helplessness. In this story it could, possibly, be literally true. When Samelweiss looks round at his colleagues after their chorus of agreement to his 'Guilty', he does so 'affectionately'. There is no reason to disbelieve the adverb there. When he refuses to let the 'corpsicle' judge introduce modern rules to his court, he does so 'reasonably'. There *is* something to balk at there, for he is refusing to let someone make a case. Still, he has reason to do so. The adverb sounds ironic to the modern reader, but under the special rules of the story it cannot be so. 'Kindly' is only one further extension of the process. Gwenanda *is* being kind in that closing speech. It is only prejudice that makes us take it in the opposite sense.

Pohl has one final device of great power throughout the story, and that is the use of 'contextless' phrases, quotations from thinkers in our own past – Hobbes, Lincoln, Disraeli, Marcus Aurelius – which continually circle the Supreme Court dome in glow-light. Would the philosophers disagree with Gwenanda and her collegues? If they would, the remarks could be directed ironically against them, and once or twice – 'The skill of making, and maintaining commonwealths, consisteth in certain rules ... not as tennis-play, on practice only', Thomas Hobbes – this seems to be the case. More often the irony is against us. Just after the first demonstration of 'summary judgement' by Samelweiss the sign lights up with:

> 'Why should there not be a patient confidence in the ultimate justice of the people? Is there any better or equal hope in the world?' – Abraham Lincoln. (p. 262)

Lincoln is normally taken as a sponsor of the present American state. But who could think that the professional legislature of today has anything to do with 'the ultimate justice of the people'? The quotation, then, can be taken as ratifying the arbitrary, amateurish, fair, and democratic Samelweiss, putting past and future in substantial alliance against the present: a process akin to some of the narrative 'disfigurements' of national myth discussed below (see pp. 107–28).

To repeat a point made earlier: though Pohl's fiction is overtly hostile to rhetoric, it still has a rhetoric of its own. The critical feature of that rhetoric, perhaps, is that while it exploits the resources of the high-informational science-fiction genre, it is also very alive – witness the use of quotations, anachronisms and voices-within-voices – to the rhetorical possibilities of *degraded* information. It is no doubt only an accident that the most recurrent science-fictional image found in this collection is that of the unreadable library and the inscrutable text (see Christie, Crossley, and Shippey on pp. 47, 88–9 and 125 below), but there is a kind of appropriateness about it just the same. It would after all be wrong to think that degraded information becomes unusable, or that the existence of degradation implies (see Meyers below) lack of faith in human power to communicate. In a way, biased narrative and altered texts tell us not only what they intend to, but also what has shaped them or formed their bias. As H. G. Wells said, apropos of his famous quarrel with Henry James, 'the Novel' consists of a frame as well as a picture. It seems particularly appropriate that the effective Father of English science fiction should have been able to claim: 'I suppose for a time I was the outstanding instance among writers of fiction in English of the frame getting into the picture.'[13] Science-fiction authors and literary readers have been in a sense re-enacting the Wells/James quarrel ever since.

The thought takes us back to questions asked at the start of this essay. Is science fiction really about modern times and modern problems, intrinsically 'referential', or has it a kind of playful or fictional autonomy? The examples given here tend to support the former view, showing clearly that in 1953 Pohl and Kornbluth were writing (with admirable foresight) about consumerism and world resources, while in 1984 Pohl had turned to questioning American law and politics, with an underlying belief that new technology could restore antique forms of elementary democracy. Some essays below confirm that view, with their demonstrations of how science fiction has coped as an exploratory mode in 'taboo' areas such as Vietnam or racialism or – one would have liked to add – gender[14] or mortality.[15] Yet it is worth noting the rather dissentient view of Alan Elms, whose study of 'Cordwainer Smith' below shows (a) that that author was not concerned with the major issue to which his 'underpeople' were connected by critics; but (b) that nevertheless his fiction did arise out of social and religious concerns of an unexpected kind; but (c) that its origins had almost nothing to do with the success of the fiction itself. Does that make *Norstrilia* (1975) or 'The Ballad of Lost C'mell' (1962) pure 'futuristic play'? The matter remains open. One can only suggest that the answer may lie not only in analyses of plot and theme, but in further painstaking probing of the special problems, in science fiction, of authorial rhetoric and readerly response: an exercise from which we have too often been distracted by the immediate, often alienating, always attention-grabbing influence of the novum.

NOTES

1 Eight different definitions are given in Ulrich Suerbaum, Ulrich Broich and Raimund Borgmeier, *Science Fiction* (Stuttgart, 1981), pp. 9–10.

2 The story is told of one of the most prominent authors of 'cyberpunk'. See further the parody 'Cy

Ber Punk's Tale', in Harry Harrison, *Bill the Galactic Hero on the Planet of Robot Slaves* (1989), for comment on science-fictional technical failings.

3 George Orwell, *Coming Up for Air* (London, 1939), cited here from the Penguin reprint of 1962.

4 See, for instance, the remark of the lower-class speaker in Eliot's *The Waste Land*, lines 219–21.

5 In my youth there was a brand of (cheap) razor-blades on sale called 'Seven O'Clock, Cock'. Seven was the time for the working class to get up, to walk or cycle to work for eight. The nine o'clock-starting middle class got up later, to catch their trains or buses.

6 Frederik Pohl and Cyril Kornbluth, *The Space Merchants* (New York, 1953), cited here from a Gollancz reprint of 1972.

7 See Darko Suvin, *Metamorphoses of Science Fiction: On the Poetics and History of a Literary Genre* (New Haven, 1979), pp. 63–84. It should be said that Suvin uses the term *novum* in a more abstract and wide-ranging way than I do here.

8 Ibid., pp. 7–8.

9 Pohl's autobiography, *The Way the Future Was* (New York, 1978), records that he was a member of the Young Communist League in the 1930s.

10 Frederik Pohl, *The Years of the City* (New York, 1984), pp. 259–334.

11 I take the term 'coloured' from the discussion of medial stages between direct and indirect speech in Norman Page, *Speech in the English Novel* (London, 1973), pp. 24–50.

12 This is another clear case of word-borrowing within

science fiction. 'Corpsicles' is an invention of Larry Niven's, prominently used for instance in his *World Out of Time* (1976).

13 H. G. Wells, *An Experiment in Autobiography*, 2 vols. (London, 1934), p. 495.

14 For an extended discussion of this issue, see Sarah Lefanu, *In the Chinks of the World Machine: Feminism and Science Fiction* (London, 1988).

15 Not much has been written on this extremely delicate taboo area, but see my article, 'Semiotic Ghosts and Ghostlinesses in the Work of Bruce Sterling' in George Slusser (ed.), *Fiction 2000: Cyberpunk and the Future of Narrative* (Ann Arbor, forthcoming 1990). Sterling is one author who does not seem convinced that people have to be mortal.

Science Fiction and the Postmodern: The Recent Fiction of William Gibson and John Crowley

JOHN R. R. CHRISTIE

Is there a postmodern science fiction? To a question posed as broadly as this, the answer has to be, yes and no. Yes, because science fiction as a fictional genre is most often placed in a notional future, and therefore attempts to be 'post' whatever modernity happens to be current. And no, because it retains the conservatism of most genre fiction, slow to change or to break with the structures and formulae which bind alike the writerly goals and readerly expectations of generic performance and consumption.

There is additionally an issue of clarification to be undertaken for the term *postmodern*. Without the addition of a suffix, the term has an unfixed status. *Postmodern* could refer to an era, the period which has succeeded the age of modernity, or it could refer to a cultural and critical category, picking out those aesthetic endeavours which somehow place themselves beyond the aesthetic paradigms of the various modernisms, of architecture, art, film, and literature. The question of science fiction and the postmodern therefore becomes a double question. Has recent science fiction, the science fiction of the 1980s, exhibited particular signs of adaptation, firstly to what economists, sociologists, and others discern as an age of *postmodernity*, and secondly, to what cultural commentators and literary critics call *postmodernism*? Despite the inertial conservatism of popular genre writing, its reliance on the boundaries which traditionally limit plot, structure, character et al., science fiction does indeed show signs of positive adaptation, both to the global postmodernity of historical process, and the postmodernism of literary and other cultural media. It does so, moreover, in ways which allow the critic to grasp at least some of the senses in which a postmodernist culture can be understood to express the preoccupations and represent the processes of an age of postmodernity.

Perhaps the 'boundaries' of genre writing, so useful for criticism's mapping exercises, are less like hermetic barriers than like the borders of territories. For it is a property of borders that, as well as demarcating, they are regularly crossed. In 1980s science fiction, I suggest, one may glimpse two processes at work. There is a quite traditional function of science fiction being quite normally fulfilled: namely the fictive exploration of emergent futures as indicated by novel technological, scientific, political, and social elements of the contemporary world. It is thus less than surprising to find science fiction's fictive discourse coinciding at certain points with the diagnostic and prognostic discourses of 'intellectuals'. Then, more significantly for the critic's interests, and perhaps more surprisingly, there is a specifically literary process whereby some science fiction writing takes on the ideological preoccupations, the stylistic registers, the formal dislocation, which might be held to characterize cultural postmodernism. It will prove possible to argue, on the basis of certain science-fiction texts, that the coincidence of subjects and themes derivative of particular perceptions of postmodernity with a literary postmodernism is not occasional and contingent, but structural and causal. If this case holds, it will validate the category of a 'postmodern science fiction', by demonstrating the integration of both connotations of postmodern, the historical postmodernity with the aesthetic postmodernism.

Part of the difficulty of this exercise is of course the lack of any consensus over what constitutes the postmodern, either historically or aesthetically. It is a much used term, whose increasingly rapid velocity of circulation tends to devalue it as linguistic currency.[1] As a historical category, nonetheless, there seems broad agreement that it marks a relatively new developmental phase of capitalism, as capitalism makes new inroads on the geopolitical globe to incorporate the Third World and now even Communist nations within its markets, and as it frees itself from two major historical constraints, the nation state and human labour. In the formal, discursive terms of political economy, postmodernity is also and obviously marked by the official adoption of a fourth order to supplement the classical triad of land, labour, and capital, to wit, information. Information in turn provides the name for the characteristic technological dimension of postmodernity: it is an age where information technology increasingly dominates archival, productive, and communicative processes, and binds them increasingly within a unifying and global network. The debates over postmodernity occur within this broad definitional consensus. Does it indicate a further turn of the oppressive screw of capitalism, or does it offer liberatory potentials? Does it presage a society rendered communally rational by the universality of its information and communication, or one where individuals become little more than information terminals, nodes for sending, switching, and receiving messages? These and other, comparable arguments between philosophers and cultural critics such as Habermas, Lyotard, and Jameson all tend to take place on the assumption that significant, perhaps fundamental shifts in economic, social, and political formations have recently occurred, whose ramifications bear strongly upon cultural practice and human subjectivity. The arguments themselves focus on the nature and implications of the change, not upon whether it has occurred.

On the cultural front, postmodernism generates a wide variety of definitions, dependent often upon which field of cultural practice is under consideration.[2] In general terms, postmodernism tends to be seen as a cultural formation where representation itself becomes established as an autonomous realm, an independent economy of signs whose power is such that it breaks down the epistemological barrier between representation and the world, between signs and referents. The image, the sign, become simulacra, no longer secondary or derivative, but primary and self-determinative, forming a surface without depth which constitutes the cultural consciousness of the age. This lack of depth, of affect, induces fragmentation, of individual and cultural identity, and the great explanatory endeavours and orderings of modernity and modernism no longer exert their powers of coherence and unification. Marx's historicism and Freud's psychoanalysis, each positing a depth of underlying powers which, when grasped, conferred intelligibility and coherence upon the epiphenomenal chaos of history, civilization, and human character, no longer command the kinds of positive and critical deference which once they did. They no longer inform cultural imagination and analysis as master-codes of understanding and practice, but rather as codes *tout court*, subsisting fragmentarily alongside other and equally plausible systems of representation, usable but not demanding to be used. Equally, postmodernism is held to leave behind modernity and modernism's primary demand, prevalent in both economic and cultural spheres, namely to make it new, to produce the novel out of the never-failing well-springs of human creativity and ingenuity. Postmodernism substitutes instead the total system of existing representational signs and forms, and seeks to create not novelty or progress, but *difference*; this it achieves by collage, bricolage, selecting, recombining, borrowing, plagiarism, pastiche – the usage in different fashion of what is already there, rather than original, *de novo* creation.

Postmodernism therefore appears to constitute itself as a series of lacks, abandonments, and absences: causal explanations, human originality, history, psyche, all recede. Or rather, the forms in which they subsisted and generated orders of meaning recede. As signs, they all persist, capable that is of producing meaning, but not under their old forms. In postmodernism, they generate meaning in the new, synchronic, and surface economy of differential signs, rather than in the old, diachronic order of human development and its deep sources. As with postmodernity, attitudes towards this cultural set can vary and polarize. A building which may mix Palladian, rococo and twentieth-century functionalist styles, and which may be, for all one can tell immediately, a bank, hotel, factory, or museum, or perhaps some combination of all of these, may strike one as a monstrous abandonment of historical, aesthetic, and social order; or it may seem an elaborately programmatic, highly erudite and self-conscious, politically liberated piece of architecture. Comparable attitudes may be taken on music which mixes the forms and instrumentation of classical and rock, or on novels which mix authenticated history and fiction, which deploy then deny sub-generic conventions, which use characters and scenes from other novels, and so forth. Postmodernist practice, in other words, can appear not just as a denial of older orders of meaning, but as a wilful, nihilistic, monstrous, or fatuous abuse of those orders. It can equally appear as art raised to hitherto unachieved levels of rigorous self-consciousness, sceptically self-questioning, aesthetically liberated, playfully ingenious. But once again, and as with all debates which are not simply a clash of incommensurables, there is a discernible level of agreement as to just what it is that receives contrary evaluations.

On the basis of the foregoing characterizations of postmodernity and postmodernism, a closer approach to the question of science fiction and the postmodern can now be made. There are a number of authors and works well-suited to such an enquiry, the most notable being Philip K. Dick. Dick, a science fiction writer of central importance and great popularity in the 1950s, 1960s and 1970s, was one of the select few to break out of the ghetto of regular science fiction readership to reach a wider audience. His fictional world, a world of schizoid, autistic, paranoid, and megalomaniac personalities, of fragmented culture, of simulacral artefact replacing nature, is one which could be held to have invented much of postmodernity and postmodernist literary practice decades before their eventual recognition and canonization by academic analysts and cultural commentators. Although his death is reliably certified by a *Times* obituary, appropriately enough for the author of such an *oeuvre*, Dick continues his existence now as a fictional entity, appearing as a character in other science fiction, and even having one novel devoted entirely to him – Michael Bishop's ironically titled *Philip K. Dick is Dead, Alas* (1988). His semiotic character persists well beyond his fleshly incarnation, a usable sign now incorporated in other codes and representational systems, subsisting there to invoke Dick's own precarious world of collapsing personalities and continually metamorphic appearances. It is, one might say, a peculiarly postmodernist fate to persist as a fictional sign mobilized in other texts, rather than to possess that immortality which conventionally arrives with literary fame. It is nonetheless a fate entirely consistent with the intent, character, and direction of Dick's work, and therefore one which, in all reason, he would have found difficult to disavow.

To provide a satisfactory treatment of Dick's fiction, even within the limits imposed by this essay's topic, is not realistically possible, so large and variegated is the body of his work. His semiotic fate can perhaps stand as one sort of complex postmodern effect within the generic field of science fiction, while his work supports a familiar science-fiction critical claim, to the effect that what general literary culture only now recognizes and expresses also rehearses the science fiction of two decades ago. Rather than treat Dick's work inadequately, therefore, this essay will examine two works of the 1980s, both well-received by readers, critics, and other science fiction authors, both indicative of science-fiction adaptation to the postmodern, in ways which both overlap and diverge, so that they indicate both the focus and the range of themes, techniques, and attitudes which inform this dimension of contemporary science fiction writing. The works under discussion are William Gibson's first novel, *Neuromancer* (1984), and John Crowely's third novel, *Engine Summer* (1979).[3]

Along many lines of comparison, these appear to be deeply antithetical works. In tone and style, Gibson's writing is a densely packed and hard-edged third-person naturalism, whereas Crowley's is a discursively rambling, warmly hued first-person, softly-toned realism. Gibson's plot is a pulp-book or popular film caper, Crowley's a traditional quest-romance. Gibson's characters are stereotypical science-fiction cardboard cut-outs, Crowley's are idiosyncratically individualized and sympathetically portrayed humans. Gibson's setting is a near-future world where the nation state has withered away and power lies with multinational corporations, where the leading edge of development is in the East not the West, and where electronic information technology has come not only to dominate forms of life recognizable to us, but to create new and increasingly unrecognizable forms of life as well. Crowley's tale is set by contrast in a relatively far, post-holocaust future, largely pastoral and inhabited by small and idiosyncratically variegated local communities.

Beyond these contrasts, however, exist common features. Both Gibson and Crowley have young male protagonists, undergoing strenuous trials and adventures, moving thereby to some kind of maturity, a standard science-fiction plot line held in place by the predominantly young male readership of science fiction. The difference between the two here is merely generational. Gibson's protagonist generates the romantic appeal of 1980s street culture, of outsider criminality, whereas Crowley's protagonist, on a quest of mythic proportions for lost and powerful objects named in the legends of his commune, inflects a hippy sensibility of the late 1960s. Even the drugs each hero uses follow this half-generational difference, Crowley's inducing tranquillity, the painless passing of time, inner clarity, whilst Gibson's requires nerve-blasting speed stimulants. To the comparability of protagonists may be added an overriding common concern to explore the significance of what one could call artefactual persons – human/machine electronic interfaces, Artificial Intelligences, machine-recorded personalities – and through this to rethink the relations of human nature and culture, of history, memory, and subjectivity. Although their methods, styles, and conclusions differ markedly, Gibson's and Crowley's novels are united in their focus upon the capabilities of this new technological interface for radically transforming the hitherto human subject. It is just this theme, namely the technologically induced mutability of subjectivity itself, which is the characteristic preoccupation of postmodern science fiction in the 1980s.

Gibson's exploration is commendably direct. He assumes a future whose two primary elements, the twin domination of a multinational capital and information technology, are by now conventional items in the listings of postmodernity. An internal feature of this environment, namely 'cyberspace', is then shown as constituting its deep structure. 'Cyberspace' is the visual image produced when one dons a headset linked into the now universal information network. In cyberspace are represented all electronic data stores, colour-coded, varying in size and brilliancy according to the density of information each contains. As a map of information, it is also a map of power and wealth. Case, Gibson's protagonist, is a new kind of criminal for this new environment. He has learned how to penetrate the defences of the data stores, and hires himself out to steal from them. At the outset, Case is in exile, his nerves biochemically burned out by employers he cheated, unable to pursue his trade. Restored to working order by a mysterious benefactor with opaque purposes, Case is able, tears streaming down his face, to achieve once more 'his distanceless home'. Cyberspace, the electronic matrix, is in other words where Case lives, moves, and has his being, a subjectivity whose essential features are formed in this human/electronic interface.

Thereafter, the plot of *Neuromancer* concerns Case's mission to liberate into autonomous existence a powerful Artificial Intelligence. In this he is aided by Molly, a razor-nailed woman of militant ferocity, Armitage, a controller and organizer, Riviera, a bio-engineered illusionist of deep perversity, Finn, an old computer expert, and Dixie Flatline, an electronic cassette recording of the cynically amusing personality and abilities of Case's one-time criminal mentor, now dead. Few of this cast's intentions and actions are of their own volition. They have been assembled by one still enchained half of the AI, who has plotted the actions necessary to unite it with its other half, thus creating the first free AI, a new form of electronic life, the first born native of cyberspace. The point about the plot is its literality. It is constituted simply by the AI's own plotting of the moves which will bring it to full being. The point about the characters is their puppet-like status, subjected to manipulation by the AI's judicious mix of inducement and compulsion. Not only are they puppet-like, they are stereotypically recognizable for science fiction readers, preceded in memory by many analogous creations.

This, however, is by no means to enter a critical note concerning Gibson's derivative and flat methods of characterization. At one moment, Case comes upon comic-book caricatures of himself and Molly. Gibson wishes us, we may take it, to realize that his two-dimensional stereotypes are intended to be just that, and must as such perform some integrated function for the narrative. Discerning this function is a significant part of discerning the postmodernist composition of *Neuromancer*. To populate his electronic postmodernity, Gibson constructs characters which are themselves flat images, beings of no psychological depth, but whose interest and significance derive from their semiotic lineage, in comic, film, pulp crime fiction, and other science fiction. They are intertextual characters, drawn from a knowing acquaintance with a wide range of contemporary popular culture. To read them critically requires not an assessment of their psychological realism, their 'humanity', but a knowledge of their semiotic descent, their always already constituted being as signs, recognizable icons within mass-marketed Western culture. In other words,

Gibson's superficiality is itself a quite meticulous compositional method, a part of his postmodernist aesthetic.

This aesthetic contains other key postmodernist elements. As Case nears the end of his mission, he finds himself amid the vast historical and cultural collections of the industrial clan of Tessier-Ashpool, at whose very heart is symbolically situated the mechanism, a jewelled, enamelled head, which will release the AI. In these collections is a library; but Case does not know what it is, for books are unknown to him, as indeed are all the historical and cultural treasures of the collection. Jumbled and juxtaposed, these artefacts of civilization are now only a residuum, recognizable for readers, but lacking meaning and content for the text's actors. In this sense, they are torn loose from history, from cultural memory, from depth of being, obliged by necessity to live in the perpetual present of electronic reality.

That reality exerts itself increasingly throughout the course of the narrative. Within it, the voice of the Dixie Flatline cassette has as much presence as the human actors, and at times more. Within it, human consciousness can be trapped within hallucinatory environments, meet and talk with electronically reconstructed dead people, with simulacral images who cannot be distinguished from their human counterparts. Cyberspace is therefore a world where image and original, sign and object, are indiscriminable, a powerful fictional representation of that dissolution of the epistemological barrier between representation and world which typifies the postmodern.

This postmodernist stance receives an intriguing modulation in *Neuromancer*'s closing scenes. The AI has been liberated, and a powerful new being, quite different from any hitherto, is loose in the world. What are the implications of this apparently apocalyptic moment in human history? The following exchange occurs between Case and the AI:

> 'So what's the score? How are things different? You running the world now? You God?'
> 'Things aren't different. Things are things.'
> 'But what do you do? You just *there*? . . .'
> 'I talk to my own kind.' (p. 270)

We have here Gibson's distinctive version of the postmodernist aesthetic of difference. The apocalyptic difference, a new order of being represented by the AI, turns out to be of little significance for human culture, a non-event. It is not merely the case then that Gibson's postmodernism characteristically chooses the pursuit of difference rather than of depth out of which to create aesthetic order and meaning. More significantly, difference-as-meaning is itself abandoned, an abandonment which coincides with the emergence of a self-conscious, intention-formulating, language-using non-human agent.

Gibson's novel can therefore be characterized, for all its apparent formularism, as a work of extremist postmodern character in its bare-faced contemplation of a technologically determined world whose culmination may be meaninglessness. His version of the postmodern is actually a rigorous posthumanism, where there is no nature, where representation constitutes the effective real, where human character is determined by cultural icon, where inhuman agents dominate; but above all, where none of this matters very much, anyway.

Gibson's posthumanist cynicism with respect to meaning is a salutary extension for postmodernism generally. It can function as a reminder that writers such as Thomas Pynchon, often regarded as central for American literary postmodernism, are often prone reflexively to privilege literary representation precisely in order to preserve the realm of representation as a haven of humanized meaning over against the intrusive advances of science and technology within contemporary culture.[4] Gibson by contrast, although on the evidence of his texts a Pynchon reader, pursues a more relentless course, constructing a minimalist paradigm of meaning through which to express the cultural implications inherent in his version of postmodernity. To his credit, there is no resort even to alienation, to characters who would be fully human if history would only allow it; his flattened characters survive if they have the skills and speed requisite in their harsh environment, where things happen too fast for regret and lamentation. Such moralized terms cannot persist in Gibson's lexical schemes, which thus complement the decline of meaning with a literal de-moralization.

Neuromancer achieves a high degree of consistency between subject, setting, character, and linguistic register. It is helped rather than restricted in this by its generically science-fiction form. Science fiction has always been written as if machinery were as or more important than persons. For science fiction, Gibson's is a familiar if extreme disenchantment; our tools and products unmake and remake us as we make them. Mainstream literature, for whatever reasons, and with odd and honourable exceptions, has found this reciprocity far more difficult to admit and express.

Engine Summer's ensemble of subject, setting, character, and style is apparently far gentler than *Neuromancer*'s. For almost all of a first reading one is conscious principally of following an artful, involving, and often beautifully written tale. The hero, Rush that Speaks, details his early life in the community of Little Belaire. A warm, enclosed society, living in seasonal rhythms, its apparent simplicity overlays a deeply thought and sophisticated system of interpersonal relations which endeavours with some success to maintain the ideal of 'truthful speaking', where one says what one means, and means what one says. Crowley's tale more or less begins, therefore, at a position opposite to where Gibson's ended. It posits the practicality of full and transparent meaning in human communication and society, a culture fully known to itself, individuals constituted in lucid intersubjectivity.

Rush, enamoured of the stories of the Saints, the founders of his community, resolves to recover the fabled, lost, and apparently magic glove and ball. He sets out to do so, encounters and lives with a kind of hermit, renews his relationship with a girl member of a tribe of travelling medicinalists, lives with this tribe for a while, and proceeds eventually to locate the glove and the ball. Shortly after, but before he returns home to his own Sainthood, the story stops.

The narrative is far more complex than the above skeletal indication. In its course, we slowly learn of the unspecified catastrophe which brought down the preceding technological civilization, of the kinds of people who survived to found new communities, of the highly advanced technological artefacts which have survived, and of a City which floats in the sky, inhabited by Angels. We gain an increasing sense of the way in which Rush's quest is patterned by these elements. We have an underlying sense of unease as we come to realize that the scene of narration is the sky-borne City, and that an Angel is both listener to the tale and interlocutor to the teller. We are by no means certain why the book's sections are called Crystals, whose facets are chapters, and are not all clear about the book's title. But we are held by dense, allusive, and graceful writing of texture, subtlety, and depth very rarely achieved in science fiction, and not often outside it.

For the reader involved with the romance tale there is always more than enough incident and context to engross attention. For the hypothetically alert postmodern reader, arguably the book's main target, there is an additional level of involvement, for two elements are thematized from the outset: meaning and narrative. Such a reader follows the tale more as a subsidiary element in a highly involuted and reflexive narrative always aware of its own status as narrative, as generation of meaning through literary artifice. Little Belaire is recognized as a society constituted by its communally shared stories. Its Saints are Saints simply in having lived lives of a density and significance which generates peculiarly memorable stories: to be a Saint is to have a Story. Thus Rush, in seeking to emulate the Saints, is in quest of his story as well as his mythical objects. True meaning, though pursued, is not guaranteed, for it may be beset by psychological anxiety and lack of self-knowledge. There is therefore at this meta-narrative level more than enough to engross the attention of such a contemporary reader.

These readings are, however, deliberately induced and carefully controlled by Crowley. They are a series of beguilements, of narrative and meta-narrative seductions performed upon the reader the more effectively to betray her. The narrative closure of *Engine Summer* finally explains any lingering puzzlement concerning the scene of narration and interlocution in the Angels' City, and also the real nature of the glove, ball, and sphere encountered by Rush on his quest. In so doing, the closure performs a deep reversal of all the narrative expectations the novel has raised, so drastically recasting the significance of both tale and meta-narrative that re-reading from the beginning, which is no longer a beginning, is enjoined.

The point of the narrative closure is that Rush's quest, and therefore his Story, is stopped before it has finished. He is about to return home bearing his objects. Will he be a Saint? Will he meet the girl again? At this point an emissary from the City descends to claim the glove, whose donning has mechanically alerted the Angels to its continuing existence. With ball, glove, and sphere the emissary takes a recording of Rush's self, his memory, personality, and Story so far. Rush returns home, probably. The recorded Rush is taken to the City. There he can be interfaced by the Angels, whose (we gather) arid and tortured existence is enriched by interpenetrating with the recorded Rush's joyful and meaningful life-story. We have been listening to the artefactual Rush, not the person. It has been there for more than half a millennium. The closing lines enact a deeply chilling inversion of the end of the Bedtime Story. It is the listening Angel who says to the storyteller: 'Ever after. I promise. Now close your eyes' (p. 182).

The frustration of the quest narrative is straightforward, for we are denied the traditional triumphal return, and fulfilment of love. The quest reader has made a mistake in believing he was reading the life of a man. He was instead reading about how a particular machine, an engine, came into being, has heard one full playing of an oft-played recording of a self, switched on and switched off like any engine. The real-time of the narrative was actually the machine-time of the engine. The punning title of the novel is clarified: *Engine Summer* equals Indian summer, the last and deceptive warmth before the chill (the seeming narrative), and also equals machine-time, the true Angelic chill of the actual narrative.

For the meta-narrative reader the challenge is more complex. Increasingly alert, let us say, to the potential complexities inherent in the scene of narration, aware of a sophisticated reflexive dimension, she will not be surprised as traditional romance closure is refused. Has Crowley's narrative sophistication deconstructed romance by this refusal? It might be so, but such a reading would have to explain why Crowley might bother to produce such an elaborate set-up for such an outworn end, and would further have to explain why the text in no way valorizes its non-completion, indeed seems to indicate its non-completion as tragic. Alternatively, is Crowley's doubled ending an example of that narrative freedom from definitive closure which postmodernist practice and criticism consistently advocates as beneficial, creating a free space for readerly involvement, refusing the representational authority of the writer? Nor can this be the case, for no such freedom exists. The master-narrative is that of the machine and its Angelic creators. This supervenes upon the romance, and definitively closes with the self-conscious machine's realization of its real and terrible condition.

It seems to be the case, therefore, that conventionally postmodernist expectations are invoked by Crowley only to be destroyed. Crowley has successfully mimicked a postmodernist textual surface of reflexive narrativity, has produced indeed a post-modern simulacrum, only to deny its validity with a genuinely tragic ending. It is a work which has produced this complex effect entirely through its structural and formal properties; but why has it done so? Crowley's focus on narrative itself is not undertaken for resolutely postmodern purposes. *Engine Summer* continuously indexes story to a series of positive human essences and values. Story, from first to last page, is equated with selfhood, with individual life, with cohesive cultural memory. It is less a literary artefact than a primary and definitional value of humanity. Put briefly, and too didactically, Crowley's point is that human lives, unlike the existence of animals or even hyper-sophisticated machines, *are stories*, with proper beginnings, middles, digressions, and ends; and that if this is so, if we lose or mistake our stories, or delegate them to other orders of being, we also lose our lives and their meanings. It is exactly this realization which constitutes the tragedy of the self-conscious machine narrator.

Still more abstractly put, *Engine Summer* can be seen to explore with both subtlety and rigour the proposition that human nature consists in more than the possession of language and self-consciousness, for the machine narrator has both these attributes, yet is not human. What it lacks, and what the original Rush possesses, is the possibility of a fulfillable narrative, a proper end.

Crowley therefore foregrounds narrativity for evidently humanist, indeed classically Aristotelian reasons, to turn the whole postmodern rhetorical apparatus of narrative and semiotic reflexivity against itself, and thereby insist that narrative is less significantly an artefact than a human essence; or rather that narrativity, the essence, is just what continually produces the artefact of narration. Crowley's technique therefore qualifies as an extremely sophisticated version of postmodern science fiction, while his adroit deconstruction of postmodern, anti-humanist expectations actually places him on classical ground.

Moreover, like Gibson, Crowley has singled out the artefactual human and the human-machine interface as the key figure of contradiction, the icon which fixes and focuses the postmodern gaze in contemporary science fiction. In their deeply contrasting styles, registers, and narrative tropes, each nonetheless expresses an equivalent concern over the emergent potentials of smart machines, and of how they might reconstitute human identity. That the two novels are among the very best of the last decade's science fiction testifies to the strength of postmodern subjects and categories in science fiction, as well as to their authors' abilities.

NOTES

1 The following discussion of postmodernity draws upon the three-cornered debate between Jean-François Lyotard, Jurgen Habermas, and Frederic Jameson. Positions are summarized in Jameson's foreword to Lyotard's *The Postmodern Condition: A Report on Knowledge* (Manchester, 1979).

2 For postmodernism, see Ihab Hassan, *The Dismemberment of Orpheus: Towards a Postmodern Literature* (London, 1971); Jean Baudrillard, *The Mirror of Production* (St Louis, 1974), and *For a Critique of the*

Political Economy of the Sign (St Louis, 1981); Hal Foster (ed), *The Anti-Aesthetic: Essays on Postmodern Culture*, (Port Townsend, Wash., 1983); and the essays by Anderson, Moretti, Jameson, Ross, Pfeil, and Holland in section III of Cary Nelson and Lawrence Grossberg (eds), *Marxism and the Interpretation of Culture* (London, 1988).

3 Page numbers in the text refer to the following editions: William Gibson, *Neuromancer* (New York, 1984); John Crowley, *Engine Summer* (London, 1982).

4 See particularly Pynchon's *The Crying of Lot 49* (Philadelphia, 1966), and the discussion of Pynchon in ch. 6 of David Porush, *The Soft Machine: Cybernetic Fiction* (New York, 1985).

Newness, Neuromancer, *and the End of Narrative*

JOHN HUNTINGTON

I

The dynamic by which science fiction discovers and defines the 'new' has been depicted by the practitioners of the genre itself as a triumph of rational art. In fact it is a much less rational process than is pictured. In addition to the usual sources of conflict that enliven any group or genre – personal envy, political disagreement, generational rivalry – science fiction, by its very nature, must create disagreement about what it is and why it is important. This special level of disagreement is particularly resistant to discussion because the rational terms by which the genre usually formulates its own importance obscure essential social dynamics of the argument and of science fiction's appeal. The argument within the genre about what is the 'new' was recently revived by the success of William Gibson's 1984 novel *Neuromancer*, which has come to typify what is now known as the 'cyberpunk' movement.[1] The novel has attracted discussion less for its plot – which tells of how Case, a dejected and self-destructive computer hacker, with the help of an extremely competent gun-for-hire, Molly Millions, breaks through the Tessier-Ashpool computer defences ('the ice') – than for its hectic imagery and its graphic vision of a world in which one can plug one's mind directly into a global computer network. Those who find the novel significantly new seem to want to read it as a serious meditation on the reality that computers will create, but their enthusiasm is not dampened when they find that Gibson does not know very much about technology. One has to suspect that *Neuromancer's* aura of newness derives from something deeper than its explicit ideas about the future.

If science fiction were as rational as it sometimes claims to be, it might make sense to argue that we cannot interpret or evaluate any claim to newness until the future depicted (whether generated by prediction, extrapolation, or some other less precise mode of foresight) has revealed itself. Such an idea contains its own refutation, for by this logic we could never discuss most science fiction, and we could never identify authentic newness until it was old. Science fiction is a *literary* genre whose value has little to do with any privileged insight into the actual future. But as soon as we have dissolved this level of paradox, we find it necessary to begin to construct anew what distinguishes science fiction from other genres. Science fiction may not be predictive, but it still engages the idea of the 'new', what Darko Suvin, following Ernst Bloch, calls the 'novum'. As Suvin carefully and exactly puts it, 'An analysis of SF is necessarily faced with the question of why and how was the newness recognizable as newness at the moment it appeared, what ways of understanding, horizons, and interests were implicit in the novum and required for it.'[2] Science fiction is less a prediction than a rendering of somebody's possibilities of hope. In interpreting science fiction we are in part analysing what an author sees as the age's potential. By interpreting the significance and the perception of newness in a work of science fiction we are entering a debate about the present historical situation. We are thinking about and debating what it is important that we think about.

We can approach this paradox-prone situation a number of ways. We can, at the simplest level, inquire about the explicit ideas in the text. Insofar as this means discussing the feasibility of machines or social organizations, such an approach quickly reaches its limit and becomes simply an assertion of political opinion. We can, however, probe deeper structures of coherence in the work. Most obviously, we can criticize the ways in which the work fails to see just how much it merely recapitulates that which it claims to transcend. In Suvin's terms, we are then showing it to be the creation of a false novum. Thus, utopias that claim gender equality but which are riddled with unconscious discriminations can be shown for what they are. Much modern science fiction, just as it has become too sophisticated to be accused of extrapolation or anticipation, seems to guard itself against such an approach by implicitly disavowing any utopian purpose and claiming futuristic *play* as an end in itself. We need to be suspicious of such a claim, however, for, as recent literary criticism has taught us, no text is simply disinterested; there is some kind of meaningful and pleasurable construct, some kind of defence, or some kind of rationalization at the heart of all fantasy. Since the text itself tries to conceal its arbitrariness and even convince itself that what it describes is natural, we can never understand this level of meaningfulness by simply accepting what the text itself says, but we must seek out the moments of strain or the irrationalities that betray repression or resistance.

Suvin asks 'why and how was the newness recognizable as newness?' To put this query in different terms, part of the difficulty we have interpreting and recognizing 'newness' derives from our inability to see the limits of our own ideologies. All writers, readers, and critics of science fiction are defined and limited by what Pierre Bourdieu calls 'habitus' and Raymond Williams calls 'structure of feeling'.[3] These are the values, expectations, and assumptions shaped by class, gender, and race, that determine our later understandings, evaluations, and actions. Bourdieu and Williams would argue that the main source of newness is the acceptance of a voice speaking out of a previously unacknowledged habitus, the introduction of new class or group values into the hegemonic canon. It is not important that new classes become the *subject* of the new literature, but that some essentially new class awareness make itself felt.

While making 'newness' its defining subject, science fiction has tended to conceal its present social interests. The technological and scientific innovations, as has already been observed, are rarely accurate to the actual future, and even if they were, they still serve mainly as rationalizations for a social fantasy. Suvin's honouring of 'valid' science fiction for its 'cognitive estrangement'[4] similarly dignifies conscious rationality without a sufficient appreciation of the political unconscious, to use Jameson's term, which underlies all literature. To return to the issue of *Neuromancer*, it seems likely that its enthusiasts find the cyberspace idea plausible, not because of any insight into future technology it entails, but because they find the 'structure of feeling' of the novel 'true' to their own sense of reality, and, by a back-formation, so to speak, they justify that feeling by finding the technology convincing.

To sketch how such a social analysis might take place, let me turn back to the beginnings of science fiction and H. G. Wells. *The Time Machine* (1895) is most revolutionary, not because it uses a scientific gesture (that Wells himself would later debunk as science) in fiction, but because it marks a small but significant shift in class allegiances. To be sure, the horror of the Morlocks can be linked to an aversion to the working classes. But that horror is somewhat of a ruse; Wells is attempting, desperately and unconsciously, to sound like a solid bourgeois. Under this superficial horror lies a more basic hostility to middle-class culture as represented by the Eloi. In all his early work Wells differs from other writers of the time and in related genres – such as Grant Allen or Arthur Conan Doyle – in his eagerness to imagine the destruction of 'civilization'. This is the expression of an anger that Wells derives from his own lower-class habitus. Thanks in large part to his confused class allegiances, Wells brings a new structure of feeling to canonic literature.

The argument for the recognition of such a deep-structural innovation is always problematic and becomes more difficult to make and to document in the case of more contemporary works. It is one thing for us to reconstruct the historical significance of *Lyrical Ballads* or *The Time Machine*, and quite another for us to evaluate a literary situation in which our own immediate structure of feeling is at risk. And any critic, in defending or resisting the work, needs to be aware that, quite apart from an evaluation of the literary or scientific 'ideas' that the work pushes to the fore, he or she is participating in the social struggle the work itself has initiated by its claim to newness. In the long run, the critic's own discussion and analysis play some role in the historical understanding and placing of the work, that is to say, in the success or failure of its social voice.

Finally, though social issues may lie at the heart of the perception of newness, we cannot begin with them. Because class is an area of struggle which literature negotiates, it is in the literature's rhetorical interests to conceal its class allegiance. Certainly *Neuromancer* does not seem explicitly concerned with class. Despite the Rastafarian connection which strongly links the novel's world with that of contemporary British punk, the world of *Neuromancer* is missing surface class dynamics. There is the Tessier-Ashpool aristocracy, of course, but that is a grotesque fantasy of incestuous isolation outside the class system altogether. The underworld that Case, Molly, and the others inhabit is a parasite to the largely invisible corporate world that produces the computer-saturated environment. The class-generated structure of feeling that we seek to uncover reveals itself, not in the concrete surface references, but in the formal structure of the work.

II

Experience in *Neuromancer* is a kind of Berkleyan sensorium in which all any character can really know is sensation. In cyberspace one *senses* just as profoundly as one does in 'real' space. Characters are intensely invested in events that they also recognize as arbitrary. Such an awareness, combining involvement and disengagement, is characteristic, not of life, but of the experience of narration. All plots are gratuitous. The Flatline construct (Case's companionable and mentoring program) puts the matter succinctly and ironically when Case tells it that he must physically invade the Tessier-Ashpool Ice, 'Wonderful . . . . I never did like to do anything simple when I could do it ass-backwards' (p. 221). Behind this joke lies a recognition of the gratuity of the plot complications that follow. To be sure, in all adventure stories the narrative is both gratuitous and a source of pleasure, but few acknowledge the former aspect so unabashedly. Wintermute, the AI, disguised this time as the bartender Ratz, says to Case, the protagonist, 'Really, my artiste, you amaze me. The lengths you will go in order to accomplish your own destruction. The redundancy of it!' (p. 234). This remark, while part of the diagesis, expresses an insight into the whole experience of the novel. This passage links the arbitrary plot to the puzzle of death, which underlies all plots. Peter Brooks, in an essay called 'Freud's Masterplot', developing ideas in *Beyond the Pleasure Principle,* explains narrative itself as a compulsive repetition leading toward death (in the case of the novel, the end, closure) and at the same time holding off death (ending, closure).[5] The double dynamic of narrative, simultaneously progressing and retarding, and its relations to the death instinct and to art are all formulated by *Neuromancer.* In pointing to the superfluity of a narrative that is also in its very superfluity engaged in a matter of life and death, the line makes clear that the meaningful and intensely contradictory relation to plot that narration usually forces on the reader in this novel belongs to the characters as well.

The equivalence of 'real' and 'matrix' experience inverts the conventional metaphors by which the mental world is understood. A number of times Gibson explains a 'real' experience by giving its equivalent in the matricial realm. What happens is an elevation of matricial hallucination and of computer competence to the level of conventional physical sensation and ability. Heroic and skilful action for Case takes place at the computer keyboard. At one important moment Molly's extraordinary athleticism is validated by being compared to the activity of a skilful computer operator: 'She went in just right, Case thought. The right attitude; it was something he could sense, something he could have seen in the posture of another cowboy leaning into a deck, fingers flying across the board. She had it: the thing, the moves' (p. 213). What is remarkable about such a passage is its exact inversion of the usual metaphors of physical grace. This subordination of the physical, and therefore of the 'real', is central to the theme of the novel.

We need to appreciate how uncommon this

theme is in the science-fiction genre. The triumph of brain over brawn, the victory of genius is, of course, a theme that has a long history in science fiction. But the complementary theme, the monstrosity of mind without body, has just as long a tradition. *Neuromancer*'s pointed emphasis on hallucination and on artificial experience would ordinarily involve this latter theme. But in this novel the empirical moralism that would denounce purely mental experience does not appear. The novel revels in surrogate experience. The computer matrix, the images of the AI, Case's reconstructed memories, even the hallucinations projected by Peter Riviera are at one level equivalent to physical experience. In such a situation 'fiction' loses its meaning because all events are fiction.

Just as the hallucinatory freedom the novel depicts renders the empirical narrative pointless, time, the dimension of tragic necessity, becomes gratuitous, merely a complication. The discrepancy between the time that Case experiences and that which the Flatline, which is unconscious when off and instantaneous when on, experiences is a recurring joke. At other times Case will experience a long adventure in the matrix and then be told by Maelcum that he has been away only five minutes (p. 245). And at another time we hear, as Case experiences the AI's facade: 'Time passed. He walked on' (p. 235). This laconic moment, by ignoring the details of duration and space that have intensely occupied the narrative's attention, reveals the artificiality and the exhaustion of the narrative itself.

One might explain such a moment as simply the failure of hack writing, but the novel is too alert, too aware of its own devices to be seen as just sloppy. The game signifies that, just as the cyberspace deck renders all experience equally artificial, the novel itself, while narrating this artificial experience from a realistic perspective, has become, by a back door, so to speak, a narrative about narrative. Though, we should hasten to add, because it posits an empirical, narratable reality, the computer matrix, as the limit of such self-reflection, the novel never becomes simply a 'postmodern' play with narrative. Wild as it is in some respects, *Neuromancer* remains true to the strong realistic narrative traditions of science fiction.

Yet even the realistic narrative here leads towards an anxious double relation. Like Stephen King, Gibson gains a kind of realism by invoking brand-names and identifying the nationality of all his technology. Unlike Stephen King's, many of Gibson's brand-names are yet to be. But, like King's domestic consumer references, which have the effect of horror just because they so anchor the reader's unnatural experience in the quotidian, Gibson's are a constant reminder of the dominated world in which the cowboy must play. Yet at the same time, these names offer pleasures, powers, and knowledges to the sophisticate. One of the deep paradoxes of high-tech consumerism is clearly apparent here: while multinational production renders us victims, there is nevertheless a *cachet* simply to knowing the technological catalogue.

An intentionally produced narrative confusion contributes to this contradiction. Gibson repeatedly refers knowingly to a futuristic machine, concept, or situation before it has been explained. Like a student in a class a little too hard, the reader finds the language being spoken always just a bit beyond comprehension, though never incomprehensible. This is, to be sure, a common science-fiction device, though it seldom occurs as regularly or as essentially as it does in *Neuromancer.* In Van Vogt, to invoke one of the first masters of the technique, we usually know when we do not know what is being talked about. Gibson puts us in a more nervous position: we usually have the anxiety that we have missed an explanation somewhere earlier. One thematic effect of the device is to imply that the reader has never grasped more than an edge of the whole reality. Such an anxiety is different from that which the characters themselves feel: they do not know some plots, but they are completely at home in the technology. This is an important discrepancy: the reader's confusion expresses a form of helplessness; the character's competence expresses a form of mastery.

Here is the central paradox of the novel: just as the novel's characters are aware of the fictional nature of their own experiences, *Neuromancer* delights in the characters' technological competence and in their (and its own) stylistic flamboyance in the midst of, perhaps even in the service of a totally dominating system. This paradox is evident in many layers of the narrative and in the theme, and one may surmise that the novel's success derives from the structural coherence that its readership experiences at this level. Stylistically, it creates anxiety about an ambiguous and oppressive reality and at the same time revels in the increased possibilities the ambiguity allows and the anarchy the oppression justifies.

III

In *Neuromancer* we are seeing evidence of a new, perhaps the final, stage in the trajectory of science fiction. If we contrast Gibson's book with the products of the genre years ago, we see a significant change in the role of the accomplished technocrat. The heroes of writers such as Heinlein or Asimov used their managerial competence to dominate their worlds. Even Van Vogt's paranoid vision allowed for mastery and triumph at the end. By contrast, Case and Robin do not dominate their world. If they pull off a caper, it is according to someone else's plan, and its consequences are not what they expected. Of course, *Neuromancer* is by no means new in its doubts about the social efficacy of technological mastery. The technological optimism of Golden Age science fiction had begun to disintegrate as early as the 1950s, and by the 1960s what is now termed the new wave challenged the dominant faith in technological solutions and tended to see us all as victims of the technocratic system. In works such as J. G. Ballard's 'The Terminal Beach' (1964) or Thomas Disch's *Camp Concentration* (1968) the scientists and technicians despair, not only about controlling or guiding their worlds, but about the very possibilities of meaning itself. The symbolic richness of the imagery of 'The Terminal Beach' is ironically empty. The protagonist's attempts to construct a symbolic centre, a concrete mandala in the desert, is trivial and vain against the onslaught of images of entropic decline (countdowns, increased sleeping time, de-evolution, dryness, depression, loss of affect). The few hints of epiphanic meaning – enigmatic messages from space voyagers, Kaldrin's mastery of multi-dimensional forms, the low-keyed erotic energy of Coma – turn out to be indecipherable and useless. *Neuromancer* shares the new wave's dark sense of the overwhelming and self-destroying system, but at the same time it breaks with new-wave pessimism by finding a positive value in the alienation of technological competence. The hacker and the game player, far from disavowing technology, glorify it and use it to compensate for the overwhelming power of the world symbolized by multinational corporations.

Such an acceptance enables a kind of guerrilla activity in the belly of the beast, but at the same time the more ecstatic its activity, the more it tends to obscure any political solution. It depicts alienation (which is something different from resistance) as a stable and permanent state. Such an attitude is indifferent to the actual politics of the system. It has resigned itself to survival on the edge, in the cracks. This is a common enough approach in life itself, but it signifies a remarkable moment in a genre which has traditionally been apocalyptic. Ironically, beneath the wild technological fantasy, we are here moving towards a kind of cynical realism.

The double consciousness of the narrative voice, aware of the artificiality of the complex plot that absorbs it, both involved and distanced, bears witness to this attitude which enjoys engagement in the wonders of technology even as it acknowledges the utter uselessness of effort. Such doubleness, which earlier phases of science fiction would have difficulty appreciating, signifies the genre's entry into a new structure of feeling. It is here, in its sympathy with the attitudes of a dominated and alienated subculture, not in its insight into actual technology or its consequences, that Gibson's novel is new. It is hard to say if the novel expresses exactly the kind of class anger that Dick Hebdige observes in British punk, but in other respects the novel sympathizes with punk's outlawry and its claim that it has chosen alienation as a significant response to the system. What appears to the science fiction tradition as political evasion may show up from this different perspective as a wise expediency. If to some readers such a road may seem a dead-end, to others it directs us to the only way to survive. A question which only time will answer is whether such narrative has a future, or whether *Neuromancer* by its success marks the end of this line of narrative exploration and thought.

NOTES

1 William Gibson, *Neuromancer* (New York, 1984). The positions concerning *Neuromancer* that are sketched in this paper are generally derived from conversation with students and with fellow participants at the conference on 'Fiction 2000' at the University of Leeds in June 1989.

2 Darko Suvin, 'SF and the Novum', in *Metamorphoses of Science Fiction: On the Poetics and History of a Literary Genre* (New Haven, 1979), p. 80.

3 'Habitus' is a key term for Bourdieu and occurs in much of his work. See especially Pierre Bourdieu, *Distinction: A Social Critique of the Judgement of Taste*, trans. Richard Nice (Cambridge, Mass., 1984), p. 101 *et passim.* Similarly, 'structure of feeling' is part of Williams's vocabulary in his early work, but see

especially Raymond Williams, *The Country and the City* (London, 1973).

4 Suvin, 'Estrangement and Cognition', in *Metamorphoses of Science Fiction*, pp. 7–8.

5 Peter Brooks, 'Freud's Masterplot', in Robert Con Davis and Ronald Schleifer (eds), *Contemporary Literary Criticism: Literary and Cultural Studies.* (New York and London, 1989), pp. 287–99.

In The Palace of Green Porcelain: Artefacts from the Museums of Science Fiction

ROBERT CROSSLEY

Recall these scenes from a short list of science-fiction masterpieces: A twenty-first-century Englishman, the last human being on earth, finds relief from loneliness by studying 'the Diorama of ages' in the monuments, libraries, and galleries of Rome. A traveller, seeking his stolen time machine, takes an afternoon off to explore the darkened corridors and ruined exhibits in a derelict museum. An unhappy mathematician feels his imagination disturbingly liberated as he walks through a preserved ancient house of the nineteenth century, 'completely enclosed in a glass shell' like an enormous museum exhibit. Ten million years from now a crew of engineers in Siberia unearths a vast underground archive of scientific and historical records carved on stone tablets by the survivors of an ancient atomic disaster. A former graduate student, having escaped a devastating plague in North America, wanders the stacks of a deserted university research library, reverently handling its books. A stowaway on an intergalactic starship is given a guided tour of the local city museum of an alien world, with special attention to a gallery of art reproductions and natural history models from Earth. In an era of profound climatic change, a pirate in a white suit hauls treasures up from the tropical waters covering the cities of Europe and installs them in his own floating museum. A visiting professor of physics from the moon, touring a museum of decorative arts in a sophisticated capital on the mother planet, sickens at the sight of a royal ceremonial garment made from the tanned skins of human beings. A self-taught reader in an illiterate future America sits in the film archive at New York University painstakingly deciphering the printed speeches of twentieth-century silent films. A visionary in a postindustrial tribal society examines the stone pillars that once supported a vanished cathedral before an atomic detonation destroyed Canterbury hundreds of years before. A twenty-first-century Australian in a world impoverished by the cumulative effects of the greenhouse phenomenon steps into the museum of Melbourne's cinematographic society and views the slapstick comedies of his great-grandparents' culture.[1]

This preliminary catalogue of artefacts from the museums, libraries, and archives of science fiction provides variants of a scene that gets reconstituted with astonishing frequency in science-fiction narratives. The spectacle of an observer examining an artefact and using it as a window on to nature, culture, and history permits that convergence of anthropological, prophetic, and elegiac tonalities that science fiction handles more powerfully than any other modern literary form. The building itself, as much as the artefact, is important in such scenes. A museum operates as a place that is at once social, impersonal, and contemplative; it also, necessarily, constitutes an artificial world that disorients spectators in space and time. As a locale, therefore, the museum is ideally suited to science fiction, that form of fantastic literature most concerned with the speculative and the epistemological, most focused on humanity at large rather than the private self, and most at home on other worlds and in times to come. When a science-fiction protagonist experiences an epiphany in a museum the event enacts in a very precise way the preoccupations of the genre itself.

Every public museum is a repository of some portion of the past and an act of faith in the future; it is a laboratory for humanistic or scientific research; it is an organized record of cultural differences and continuities; it stands as a secular and populist alternative to the private collections of churches and social elites. Similarly, science fiction is specially concerned with temporality and change, with the representation and analysis of cultural difference, with experimental constructions of hypothetical realities, with the intersections of natural history and human history, and with the development of countercultural and popular audiences; in all these respects it has functional affinities with the museum. Above all, both the museum and the science-fiction text have a paradoxical relationship to time. 'Virtually all the best science fiction is, explicitly or implicitly, a kind of time travel,' one recent historian of the genre has argued.[2] The same might be said of the best museums. A museum is never wholly a monument to the past any more than science fiction is narrowly or exclusively a literature of the future; while the museum typically represents the past (even if only the *recent* past), its interest in preservation makes it profoundly committed to the future, and while science fiction is usually oriented to the future it rarely looks ahead without also glossing the present and the past. A museum may not be precisely a time *machine*, but it is a contrivance that collapses linear time and encourages the tourist who visits it to shuttle back and forth imaginatively among temporal worlds. Before looking more closely at the uses of such temporal disjunctions in a few of the fictional scenes in museums summarized in my preliminary list, I want first to sketch a very brief institutional history of the museum as it bears on the aesthetic concerns of science fiction.

The opening of museums as public buildings rather than private 'cabinets of curiosities' roughly parallels the historical rise of science fiction. Both the public museum and the genre of science fiction are emblems of the nineteenth century's experiment in the democratization of culture. It is true that one may find suggestive anticipations of science fiction in Lucian or Milton or Swift, and so too there are prefigurings of the modern museum in ancient and Renaissance collections of natural objects and cultural artefacts. Nevertheless, most historians of science fiction find the genre achieving its authentic identity only in the nineteenth century – either with Mary Shelley if you follow Brian Aldiss's account of Gothic origins or somewhere in the latter third of the century if you accept Mark Rose's argument that the genre is emphatically postromantic[3] – and similarly most cultural historians see the public museum as essentially a nineteenth-century creation. Ancient collections with limited access like those housed in the Library at Alexandria were more akin to the private holdings of the royal houses of Europe than to the museums and libraries of the past two centuries. The treasure hoards of feudal lords have far more in common with the contemporary market for 'collectibles' as a form of investment than with the museum's functions of conservation, arrangement, and public display of artefacts. Of other possible prototypes for the modern museum the most viable is the medieval cathedral which in its architecture and crafts (if not always in its manuscripts and art treasures) could make limited claims to be 'people's buildings', open to all.[4]

When the first London College of Antiquaries was founded in 1572 its members celebrated their personal collections of rarities – often the loot from so-called voyages of discovery – more as trophies of wealth and as hobbies to be shared with fellow antiquarians than as bases for museums of science or of art; but in the eighteenth century a reformed Society of Antiquaries began to articulate the principles on which future public museums would be established. Collectors of scientific and artistic curiosities, the Society maintained in initiating its journal *Archaeologia* in 1770, might help prevent the darkness of ignorance from descending on a future age:

> The only security against this and the accidents of time and barbarism is, to record present transactions, or gather the more ancient ones from the general wreck. The most indistinct collection has this merit, that it supplies materials to those who have sagacity or leisure to extract from the common mass whatever may answer useful purposes.[5]

By the end of the eighteenth century the connoisseur was in the ascendancy over the indiscriminate collector, although not every putative rarity could live up to the Society's grand claims. The century could boast Sir Hans Sloane's extraordinary 100,000 specimens that eventually formed the core collection of the British Museum, but there were also such whimsical sideshows as Pontius Pilate's wife's chambermaid's sister's hat in the collection of James Salter – a useful reminder that the connoisseur and the con artist often roam the same territory.[6] But the Society of Antiquaries, while championing the scholarly value of even 'the most indistinct' of its members' holdings, was not proposing to open the collections to any but those few suitable people of 'sagacity or leisure'.

The Ashmolean is widely recognized as the first modern museum, in which natural history specimens, antiquities, and various 'curiosities' were arranged for display, for teaching, and for public inspection at a charge of sixpence, so that country folk arriving in Oxford on market-day could crowd in to examine Roman burial urns, St Augustine's crozier, or the famous stuffed dodo.[7] In fact, the *Oxford English Dictionary*'s first two recorded usages of 'museum' in its modern sense of 'a building or portion of a building used as a repository for the preservation and exhibition of objects' are references to the Ashmolean.[8] But the Ashmolean was not typical of eighteenth-century museums, and its location in a university town ensured that its primary audience would be scholarly. The British Museum, established in 1759, took nearly a century to begin to admit the public in significant numbers on a regular basis.[9] The model public art museum in the early nineteenth century was the Louvre – which managed to combine the populist principles of the

Revolution with the rich plunder gathered up during the Napoleonic wars – and the Pennsylvania Academy of Fine Arts had similar intentions of being a 'people's palace'. But London took several decades to catch up with these democratic tendencies. The reopening of the British Museum in 1829 at its new location in Bloomsbury, the completion of the domed reading-room in 1857, and the siting of the Natural History, the Science, and the Victoria and Albert Museums in South Kensington in the second half of the century are vital signs of the coming of age of the English public museum. The dramatic potential for the emerging museum as a locale in science fiction can be illustrated by comparing two nineteenth-century futurist texts, one published when the fascination with museums was just beginning to catch the public imagination and one published later when museums were enjoying their heyday.

The final scenes of Mary Shelley's 1826 eschatological novel *The Last Man* are played out in the palaces and churches of Italy as Lionel Verney and a diminishing circle of companions seek consolation for the impending extinction of humanity by contemplating 'master-pieces of art', 'galleries of statues', and other 'antiquities'.[10] Arriving in Venice, the survivors climb the tower of San Marco for a prospect view of the tumbledown condition of the city's famous buildings, the paintings defaced by salt water and mud, and the seaweed draped over marble artefacts. 'In the midst of this appalling ruin of the monuments of man's power,' Verney writes with romantic gloom, 'nature asserted her ascendancy, and shone more beauteous from the contrast' (p. 319). Alone after the deaths of his last two companions during a storm, Verney takes a grim satisfaction in imagining how, if the earth should ever be repopulated by some other intelligent species, our artefacts might offer a window on to human civilization and 'we, the lost race, would, in the relics left behind, present no contemptible exhibition of our powers to the new comers' (p. 331).

The last man's ultimate destination is Rome, 'the capital of the world, the crown of man's achievements' (p. 335). Its 'storied streets, hallowed ruins, and stupendous remains' (p. 335) make the whole city *the* great outdoor exhibit of European culture. Wandering among the sculptures of Phidias and Praxiteles, touring the Coliseum and the temple of Jupiter, Verney wants to validate the grandeur of human aspiration and achievement. But when he sees a buffalo walking along the ancient Roman avenues he understands that the age of human dominance is gone, that already other creatures have begun to occupy the space we called 'Rome'. He takes to sheltering in an abandoned palace, where he can pass his sleepless nights with splendid paintings; in a Keatsian gesture he embraces and kisses the cold marble of statues representing passionate lovers; and mimicking papal pomp he solemnly ascends the steps of St Peter's to carve the numbers 2100 in stone, the date of humanity's last year. In the absence of any social context, both the artefacts and the beholder appear ludicrous or pitiful. At the end Verney harbours no more illusions about 'eternal Rome'; he feels himself a living anomaly, his body 'a monstrous excrescence of nature' (p. 340), and Rome becomes both physiologically and psychologically a deathtrap: a breeding-place for malaria and a shrine to the dead-end of human aspiration.

Few of the buildings Shelley's Verney visits can be called properly 'museums'. The power of this climactic scene resides in its focus on monuments, urban architecture, and artefacts which belong to the public perception, even myth, of imperial and ecclesiastical Rome. It is Verney's consciousness rather than the design of a curator that organizes these disparate artefacts and displays them to the reader as a lesson in the glory and the boundaries of artistic achievement. When H. G. Wells attempted a similar didactic episode seventy years later in *The Time Machine* (1895) he was able to do so with greater concentration and a more impressive art because he could draw upon the idea of the public museum and the experience of museum-goers in ways not quite yet available to Shelley. 'At the first glance,' the time traveller recalls of his stepping through the main door of a still-imposing though disused building 800 millennia from now, 'I was reminded of a museum.'[11] The familiarity of the design of its entrance ('the customary hall, a long gallery lit by many side windows') leaves him in no doubt about the building's purpose and signals to the reader that the function of this episode will be in some way analogous to our familiar museum experiences. In this instance, as in many others in the early history of science fiction, Shelley and Wells seem almost to work in tandem: she pioneering an intellectual strategy and he discovering its most streamlined narrative form; she articulating the archetype and he imagining the fictional prototype. If Shelley found a way to turn all Italy into a museum as a way of fabricating a *memento mori* for the human species, Wells succeeded in creating the most memorable of all science-fictional museums, the eerie, deserted, ruinous Palace of Green Porcelain.

Inside that vast structure of metal, glass, and tile the traveller explores galleries of palaeontology, mineralogy, botany, zoology, chemistry, military history, ethnography, industrial history, and many others unspecified in the course of a long and wearying afternoon. Excepting some sketchily described futuristic machines in one gallery, all of the exhibits might have been found in London in 1895. Wells's Palace is almost certainly a composite of the several branches of the British Museum in Bloomsbury and South Kensington as they existed at the close of the nineteenth century. In uniting these separate buildings into one 'Palace' Wells accomplished in fiction and in the future what Prince Albert dreamed of at mid-century: a single grand institution that would acknowledge the interdisciplinary nature of anthropological study and that would not separate natural history from human artefacts in the study of culture. Surviving photographs suggest that some details of Wells's Palace are drawn directly from the Victorian museums he knew: the enormous fossil of a brontosaurus at the entrance to the Palace is reminiscent of the brontosaurus that dominated the East Dinosaur Gallery of the Natural History Museum and 'the old familiar glass cases of our time' duplicate those that the trend-setting British Museum had just installed in its ethnographic galleries. The cracked and smashed 'white globes' the traveller sees hanging from the ceiling of an interior gallery undoubtedly reflect the recent installation of electrical lighting in the buildings at Bloomsbury and South Kensington.[12]

Many commentaries on *The Time Machine* either ignore this chapter, or view it as a kind of interlude in the narrative,or give it short shrift as a supply depot out of which the traveller can arm himself to recover his machine and so advance the plot to its proper culmination in the year thirty million.[13] But Wells and his traveller have to go out of their way to get to the Palace of Green Porcelain – eighteen miles the traveller estimates – and there may have been more convenient ways to get fire and a club into the time traveller's hands if that was all Wells was after. The Palace is a locale central to the aesthetic and moral design of *The Time Machine*, I suggest, because Wells saw the institution of the museum as an immediately accessible icon for the narrative's philosophical concerns with nature and culture, time and change. In what he calls 'this ancient monument of an intellectual age' the traveller, alternately exhilarated and dismayed, receives a vision of mortality, of the inexorable processes of time, of the frailty of human culture second in power only to his more famous apocalypse in the year thirty million. If that later vision of the world's end offers the definitive view in *The Time Machine* of the hostility of the cosmos to terrestrial life, the epiphany in the Palace of Green Porcelain is the book's most concentrated lesson in the vanity of human wishes and the brevity of mind.

Any catalogue of artefacts from science fiction's many museums would have to give pride of place to the contents of Wells's Palace: the sealed camphor and matches, the bulky corroded machinery, the Eloi necklaces fashioned out of fossilized bones, the dummy dynamite caps, the inoperable guns, and the easily vandalized stone idols arranged in what the time traveller names 'the ruins of some latter-day South Kensington'. But the most spectacular moment in the Palace of Green Porcelain comes when the traveler enters a room hung with 'brown and charred rags'. At first mistaking them for decayed military banners, he quickly grasps that he has happened upon the museum's library and that the rags are what survive of its books. Staring at the empty bindings, he wryly places the fate of his own seventeen published scholarly papers on optics into the framework of a universal disintegration of texts: 'They had long since dropped to pieces, and every semblance of print had left them. But here and there were warped boards and cracked metallic clasps that told the tale well enough. Had I been a literary man I might, perhaps, have moralized upon the futility of all ambition.' In his epiphany in the museum Wells's traveller, not for the last time in the narrative, marks the end of a world. The 'sombre wilderness of rotting paper' in the Palace's library furnishes an elegiac commentary on the fantasy of the triumph of will over time, of art over nature. Precisely because the time traveller does not speak out of the wishful sensibilities of 'a literary man', the episode amounts to a matter-of-fact repudiation of the bravado that opens Shakespeare's fifty-fifth sonnet:

> Not marble nor the gilded monuments
> Of princes shall outlive this pow'rful rhyme.

Tellingly, what survive best in the Palace are the means for destruction – sulphur and camphor and matches, rusty hatchets and a mechanical lever recycled into a mace; the works of intellect and imagination are only as durable as their materials.

Poetry, philosophy, criticism, scholarly journals, scientific romances, the printed words you are reading right now: these are far more fragile.

Wells's successor as historian of the future, Olaf Stapledon, imagined more durable textual artefacts surviving time's processes, but foresaw an equivalent fragility in the mental and moral stability of future users of the materials preserved from the past. One entire stage of *Last and First Men* (1930) can be described in terms of a pair of crucially placed archives. Stapledon's Patagonians, struggling to contrive a human civilization some 100,000 years from now, are psychologically devastated when a team of archaeologists discovers in the basement of a derelict building in China metal plates from which twentieth-century books were printed. Decoding this futuristic Rosetta Stone, Patagonian linguists and cultural anthropologists realize that their own culture, at a stage roughly equivalent to the European Renaissance of the sixteenth century, had been long since surpassed and that their human ancestors had not been primitive but highly and dangerously developed. Everything the Patagonians thought they were discovering and inventing was in fact a recovery. Some of them find this revelation a deterrent to initiative and become reactionaries incapable of facing the future because paralysed by the past: others take the evidence of a lost high civilization as reason to hope that such a level of material comfort and intellectual vigour might be achieved again.

In the upshot this 'progressive' mentality wins out, though the triumph is as problematic and as compromised as that of our familiar twentieth-century progress. The Patagonians restore civilization at the price of nationalism, global warfare, economic rivalries, class stratification, squandering of planetary resources, and at last the unleashing of the djinn in the bottle of atomic energy. A chain reaction scalds the planet and destroys all but thirty-five members of the human species, and thus the ruined Chinese depository of printing blocks predicts the cycle of human risings and fallings central to the aesthetic and psychological design of *Last and First Men*; the artefacts miraculously preserved from the twentieth century serve only to stimulate the cataclysm of the hundred-thousandth century. Out of that cataclysm the survivors in Siberia, before sinking after several generations into subhuman barbarism, create a stone archive preserving as much knowledge of the Patagonian civilization as they can on carved tablets, along with a pictorial dictionary and grammar. The project falters when newer generations begin to resent 'the hardship of engraving endless verbiage upon granitic slabs'.[14] Inevitably, several million years later, that stone museum is unearthed, its artefacts decoded, and its ideals recycled into the evolved human species Stapledon calls the Second Men. The condition of the literary artefacts in Wells's Green Palace and the uses made of the historical records removed from Stapledon's archives testify to both the grandeur and the ironies in the human project of composing imperishable monuments, whether in stone, in metal, or in words.

In George Stewart's *Earth Abides* (1949) the library at the University of California at Berkeley has a similarly pivotal role in defining an attitude toward civilization. Initially Isherwood Williams cherishes the library as a cultural temple and a bulwark against a reversion to barbarism in the aftermath of a global epidemic. 'Here rested in storage the wisdom by which civilization had been built, and could be rebuilt', we are told after Ish carefully breaks into the building.[15] But as a new arcadian society forms, the library's treasures, at first invested with a taboo status by Ish, come to seem largely irrelevant to the future. Books, after all, will be 'mere wood-pulp and lampblack' (p. 268) in an unlettered culture. When a great fire burns most of the San Francisco Bay area near the end of the novel, the elderly Ish observes among the gutted buildings of the university campus the still-intact library, its million volumes amazingly spared from the flames. He feels he should rejoice in this preservation but is no longer sure that the accumulated wisdom of earlier ages will matter to the future. Guiltily, he turns his back on the literary and scientific culture embodied and entombed in the library: 'Will I dream of a million books passing in endless procession, looking reproachfully upon me because after so long I have begun to have doubts in them and all they stood for?' (p. 309).[16]

As Ish stands in the reader's near future pondering a more distant future he loses confidence in the ability of a bankrupt past to offer any usable guidance for those who will shape the new society. 'History repeats itself,' according to one of the central aphorisms in *Earth Abides* , 'but always with variations' (p. 176), and therefore the relation of past and future will always be problematic. In a later post-catastrophe novel which imagines a less attractive illiterate society than the neo-Amerindian one Stewart projected, Russell Hoban has staged an epiphany in the closest thing to a museum in south-eastern England to survive the nuclear holocaust that ended twentieth-century civilization. At 'Cambry Senter' the latterday mystic Riddley Walker discovers a crypt that once sat beneath Canterbury Cathedral. Entering the hole in the ground where, as it seems to him, stone trees grow out of the earth, he is shaken by his perception of a saner ancient world whose artisans carved pillars with such cunning art and out of an instinctive sense of the wholeness of things:

> it come to me what it wer wed los. It come to me what it wer as made them peopl time back way back bettern us. It wer knowing how to put ther selfs with the Power of the wood be come stoan. The wood in

the stoan and the stoan in the wood. The idear in the hart of every thing.

If you cud even jus only put your self right with 1 stoan. Thats what kep saying its self in my head. If you cud even jus only put your self right with 1 stoan youwd be moving with the girt dants of the every thing the 1 Big 1 the Master Chaynjis. Then you myt have the res of it or not. The boats in the air or what ever. What ever you done wud be right.

Them as made Canterbury musve put ther selfs right. Only it dint stay right did it. Somers in be twean them stoan trees and the Power Ring they musve put ther selfs wrong.[17]

In *Riddley Walker* (1980) these relics from medieval culture outline the tragedy of Riddley's world and ours but they also define the aesthetic of the artefact Riddley is making as he struggles with a degenerate language to write the autobiographical and anthropological narrative that we read, a text in which Riddley attempts to put himself – and the world – right again.

In Arthur C. Clarke's *Childhood's End* (1953) the epiphany takes place on another world, although as in *The Time Machine* from the moment the protagonist enters the alien building of the overlords there is no doubt in his mind that the structure must be a museum. The stowaway Jan Rodricks, stunned by the radical strangeness of daily life on another planet, gets 'a much needed psychological boost to find himself in a place whose purpose he could fully understand'.[19] But if he finds the physical layout of the interstellar museum familiar and reassuring, Jan does not find his actual tour of the museum an antidote to culture shock. Far from it. In an interview with the Curator for Earth he is distressed at how few of the terrestrial specimens he can identify and at the magnitude of his ignorance of human culture. His pride chastened, he then is given a further jolt when he sees the model of an enormous eye of a 'cyclopean beast' from a distant stellar system (p. 197), an eye so frighteningly alien that it further reduces the stature of human beings in the midst of a Nature infinitely inventive and profoundly inhuman.

J. G. Ballard's *The Drowned World* (1962) is enacted on our own planet but its physical environment is in many ways as alienating as anything in *Childhood's End* . The most spectacular site in *The Drowned World* is the submerged London planetarium to which the biologist Robert Kerans descends in diving gear, but the essential museum locale in the novel may be Strangman's 'treasure ship', a mobile monument to kitsch and rapacity. Strangman, the leader of a gang of vandals who plunder the abandoned cities of Europe, has installed meretricious pseudo-art in the form of fake marble columns, peeling gilt banisters, gold-coloured draperies and tassels that, we are told, give the ship's decor the look of 'a bad film set of Versailles'. [19] The ship's cataloguing room contains a miscellany of good and bad pieces looted from museums: stone limbs and torsos, an ornamented altarpiece, stacks of gilt-framed pictures, pairs of huge cathedral doors, pieces of armour, equestrian statues, ceremonial inkstands, and other assorted bric-a-brac. Strangman, walking his visitors through the storeroom, identifies this mass of stuff with a single identifying phrase about its original home: 'Sistine Chapel' or 'Medici Tomb'. One of the tourists on this pirate ship murmurs, 'Aesthetically, most of this is rubbish, picked for the gold content alone' (p. 93). Another member of the party says of the museum relics simply, 'They're like bones' (p. 93). And two black sailors from Strangman's crew turn this into a derisive chant: 'Bones! Yes, man, dem's all bones! Dem bones dem bones dem . . .!' (p. 94).

Strangman, as Mark Rose has indicated, is the pivotal figure in *The Drowned World*, and his project to drain the water from London and re-expose the artefacts from the city's lost museums is a ghoulish activity.[20] The museums in Ballard's narrative are the tombs of the past, and the effort to reclaim the past – whether by acquisitive madmen like Strangman or by Kerans's scientific expedition into the sunken planetarium – leads to revulsion, nightmare, and flight. Ballard's museums, presided over by the spookily elegant skeletons of Delvaux paintings and the surreal images of Max Ernst, have an elegiac function like the Palace of Green Porcelain, the Rome of *The Last Man* , and the ruins of Canterbury Cathedral, though where Wells, Shelley, and Hoban emphasize the achievements that have been lost, Ballard highlights (even more emphatically than George Stewart) the dilapidation of Western culture and (with Clarke) dramatizes the alienation of the museum visitor from the artefacts. Ballard's science-fictional museum becomes either a sterile memento of a world well-drowned as in the underwater planetarium or a cultural rummage in which artistic accomplishment is inextricably linked with vulgarity, robbery, and racism.

I end as I began with Wells and Shelley. Almost the time traveller's last act in the Palace of Green Porcelain, a gesture that from one perspective is the most trivial in the whole narrative, occurs when museum-fatigue has left him with a waning interest in the silent galleries he has been exploring. He enters a room full of ancient totems from a great cross-section of planetary cultures and pauses before a massive figure carved in soapstone: 'And here, yielding to an irresistible impulse,' he says, 'I wrote my name upon the nose of a steatite monster from South America that particularly took my fancy.' This piece of apparently gratuitous vandalism, this desire to announce his presence and even to claim possession of the artefact not only makes an incongruous link between Wells's self-consciously proper Victorian and Ballard's sleazy Strangman, it also stands as one of the most provocative commentaries on the recurrence of museums in science fiction. Wells's traveller, anonymous to us, in an act of mischief carves his signature into an ancient artefact encountered 800,000 years from now. Every reader of *The Time Machine* remembers the pair of flowers the traveller brings back from the future to his dinner guests in 1895, but the impulse to leave behind some graffiti in 802,701 is an equally eloquent – and perhaps a more revealing – gesture. Although no one will ever read it, the traveller cannot forgo the self-important announcement that Kilroy was here. Mary Shelley's Lionel Verney does much the same sort of thing in his final days, getting white paint from a deserted shop and, as he makes his way toward Rome, inscribing his name in three languages on a conspicuous place in each town he passes through: 'Verney, the last of the race of Englishmen'. Beneath this flamboyant obituary, he adds as postcript, this time only in Italian, a more homely *cri de coeur* addressed to the figment of another survivor: 'Deh, vieni! ti aspetto!' [Come, I beg you. I am waiting for you!] (p. 332).

To these self-focusing flourishes we might add Ish's discovery of his own name written on the check-out slip of a book on geography in the Berkeley library (p. 268), Kerans's startled vision of himself in a mirror in *The Drowned World*'s planetarium (p. 106), and Jan Rodricks's irrational and overwhelming conviction that that single, gigantic, artificial eye is staring at *him* (p. 196). In all these instances we are reminded that in the showcases of science fiction's museums *we* are what is chiefly on display. The artefacts in the museums may be historical, extraterrestrial, or futuristic, may be the most elegant products of a refined civilization, the unfathomable evidences of a totally alien mind, the shameful testimony of human crimes, the poignant relics of a vanished splendour, or junk indiscriminately preserved by time's accidents. Whatever its source, whatever the predilections or deficiencies of its curators, the science-fiction museum invites the reader to become a tourist and to peer into the glass case in wonder and often in alarm at an object that collapses distances of time and space, disorients and displaces the observer, and ultimately requires us to put ourselves right again. Such curiosity, disorientation, estrangement, and altered perception is a sequence the reader of works in this most modern of fictional genres frequently undergoes. Certainly in science fiction's museums, if we look long enough, we will at last and almost inevitably see with unmistakable clarity an object inscribed not only with Kilroy's name but with ours.

NOTES

1 The events summarized come from these novels, in order: Mary Shelley, *The Last Man* (1826); H. G. Wells, *The Time Machine* (1985); Yevgeny

Zamyatin, *We* (1924); Olaf Stapledon, *Last and First Men* (1930); George Stewart, *Earth Abides* (1949); Arthur C. Clarke, *Childhood's End* (1953); J. G. Ballard, *The Drowned World* (1962); Ursula K. LeGuin, *The Dispossessed* (1974); Walter Tevis, *Mockingbird* (1980); Russell Hoban, *Riddley Walker* (1980); and George Turner, *The Sea and Summer* (North American title: *Drowning Towers*) (1987).

2 Karl Kroeber, *Romantic Fantasy and Science Fiction* (New Haven, 1988), p. 27.

3 See the opening chapters of Brian Aldiss, *Trillion Year Spree: The History of Science Fiction* (New York, 1986), pp. 25–52 and Mark Rose, *Alien Encounters: Anatomy of Science Fiction* (Cambridge, Mass., 1981), pp. 1–23.

4 On the development of the modern science museum out of private libraries and 'cabinets of curiosities' see Silvio A. Bedini, 'The Evolution of Science Museums', *Technology and Culture*, 6 (Winter 1965), pp. 1–29. Alma S. Wittlin chronicles the emergence of the 'public service' function of the museum in *The Museum: Its History and Its Tasks in Education* (London, 1949).

5 'Introduction', *Archaeologia, or Miscellaneous Tracts Relating to Antiquity, Published by the Society of Antiquaries of London*, vol. I (1770), p. ii.

6 On the collections of Sloane and Salter see Arthur MacGregor, 'The Cabinet of Curiosities in Seventeenth-Century Britain', in Oliver Impey and Arthur MacGregor (eds), *The Origins of Museums: The Cabinet of Curiosities in Sixteenth-and Seventeenth-Century Europe* (Oxford, 1985), pp. 147–58. See

also Michael Hunter, 'The Cabinet Institutionalized: The Royal Society's "Repository" and Its Background', also in Impey and MacGregor, pp. 159–68.

7 Reports of early tourists to the Ashmolean, including continental scholars scandalized by the open-admissions policy, are cited in Martin Welch, 'The Ashmolean as Described by its Earliest Visitors' in Arthur MacGregor (ed.), *Tradescant's Rarities: Essays on the Foundation of the Ashmolean Museum, 1683*, (Oxford, 1983), pp. 59–69.

8 Useful discussions of the early history of the word *museum* in English appear in Wittlin, *The Museum*, pp. 1–8 and in Hunter's appendix to 'The Cabinet Institutionalized' in Impey and MacGregor, *The Origins of Museums*, p. 168.

9 On discontent in the 1820s over limited public access to the British Museum's collections and reading-room, see Edward Miller, *That Noble Cabinet: A History of the British Museum* (London, 1973), pp. 122–4.

10 Mary Shelley, *The Last Man*, introd. Brian Aldiss (1826; rpt, London, 1985), p. 313. Further references to this edition are given parenthetically.

11 H. G. Wells, *The Time Machine: An Invention* (London, 1895), ch. 11. The 16-chapter format of the first edition was later altered to a 12-chapter format, often adopted in later reprintings; in the latter, the episode of the museum falls in chapter 8. All citations in this essay are from chapter 11/8.

12 Kenneth Hudson discusses Prince Albert's ideal of a unified museum in *Museums of Influence* (Cambridge,

1987), pp. 69–70. Photographs on pp. 27 and 71 show, respectively, the new glass cases at the British Museum and the brontosaurus skeleton in the Museum of Natural History.

13 In *The Definitive Time Machine: A Critical Edition of H. G. Wells's Scientific Romance* (Bloomington, Ind., 1987), Harry M. Geduld sees the visit to the Palace as an 'autonomous' episode in which Wells 'is depicting scenes rather than developing plot' (p. 12). My own earlier commentary on the Palace in *H. G. Wells* (Mercer Island, Wash., 1986) treats it only as a place where the traveller 'procures weapons' (p. 26). An important exception to this general neglect is John Huntington's account of the visit to the museum as an instance of Wells's mediation of opposites in *The Logic of Fantasy: H. G. Wells and Science Fiction* (New York, 1982), pp. 46–7.

14 Olaf Stapledon, *Last and First Men* (1930; rpt. New York, 1968), p. 95.

15 George R. Stewart. *Earth Abides* (1949; rpt. New York, 1971), p. 116. Further references to this edition are given parenthetically.

16 Ish's wistfulness about the good old days is countered throughout the novel by Em, the new Eve of the emergent arcadian society, who indicts the failures of the Euroamerican imagination. As a women and an African-American, Em refuses to mourn the lost cultural literacy of the past, makes mordant observations on the 'communication' that resulted from European voyages of exploration to Africa and the Americas (p. 174), and derides the vindictive male God of Judaeo-Christian tradition (p. 258).

Artefacts from the Museums of Science Fiction

17 Russell Hoban, *Riddley Walker* (1980; rpt. New York, 1982), pp. 161–2.

18 Arthur C. Clarke, *Childhood's End* (1953; rpt. New York 1974), p. 194. Further references to this edition are given parenthetically.

19 J. G. Ballard, *The Drowned World* (1962; rpt. Harmondsworth, 1965), p. 92. Further references to this edition are given parenthetically.

20 See Rose's superb commentary on *The Drowned World* in *Alien Encounters*, pp. 127–38.

The Fall of America in Science Fiction

TOM SHIPPEY

The picture on the cover of the December 1966 issue of *Fantasy and Science Fiction (F&SF)* is of the Statue of Liberty, recognizable immediately by its raised arm, seven-pronged diadem, and severely expressionless features. Yet the statue is lying on or rather in the ground, from which it appears to have been recently excavated. A small human figure in singlet and trunks stands by its lip, its gestures vividly conveying incomprehension. Four others look on in poses of doubt or inquiry. What this picture means is on one level obvious enough: this must be a scene from the future, indeed the far future, in which the Statue of Liberty has been not only felled and buried, but also forgotten, so thoroughly forgotten that the future excavators, whoever they are, can no longer even guess the purpose of the artefact they have discovered. The meaning of this cover is the precariousness of meaning, the evanescence of that which most Americans would take to be most solid, most eternal.

The device is a common one with science fiction

illustrators. But it is worth considering quite how covers of that kind *create* meaning, perhaps especially in comparison with the 'mythical' effects created by the cover of *Paris-Match* as memorably analysed by Roland Barthes in *Mythologies.*[1] In his discussion of 'myth as a semiological system' in that work, Barthes describes a cover-picture on which 'a young Negro in a French uniform is saluting with his eyes uplifted, probably fixed on a fold of the tricolour.' What does this mean to Barthes? His answer is to say that we are dealing here with two overlapping systems, each consisting of a signifier, a signified, and a sign, but in which the sign of the first or linguistic system (a sign being the combination of signifier and signified) becomes in its turn the signifier of the second or mythical system, with a different signified and a different sign. Viewed as the final term of the first system, the *Paris-Match* cover means no more than has already been said, 'a Negro is giving the French salute.' But as the first term of the mythical system, the cover prompts a whole train of thoughts about 'French imperiality', its essential rightness, the delusions of those who criticize it, the loyalty of those who serve it, etc. That is what the cover was designed to do, Barthes points out. He points out also, with almost equally evident rightness, that as the cover's mythical meaning gains force, point, appropriateness, so it *loses* individuality, biography, even story. The young Negro whose picture was taken must have had a nationality, as well as a life-history, of his own. But in the context of 'imperiality' (the salute, the uplifted eyes, the hypothesized tricolour in the background) all that is just not relevant. The only important thing about him is that he should be visibly 'not-French'; that his pose and skin-colour should apparently contrast, to be resolved by the ideology of 'imperiality'. The linguistic and the mythical systems can alternate, says Barthes:

> the signification of the myth is constituted by a sort of constantly moving turnstile which presents alternately the meaning of the signifier and its form, a language-object, and a metalanguage, a purely signifying and a purely imagining consciousness.[2]

Does this work with science fiction? It is very tempting to remark that what in Barthes is seen as the end-product of mythical decoding for *Paris-Match*, is for the reader of *F&SF* only the start: to understand the full significance of the Statue of Liberty cover one has to see *first* that the Statue has a mythical significance like that of the Negro soldier, and *then* to see that this significance is being denied. Furthermore the act of working out how that could get to be denied – the Statue is buried, the United States must have collapsed, the very concept of liberty must have lost importance – leads one in the direction of inventing a story,[3] so pouring back into the picture all the individuality, biography and detail leeched from the 'French Negro picture' (according to Barthes) by the process of mythification itself. The *Paris-Match* cover is a myth, one might say, the *F&SF* cover is a 'myth disfigured'.[4] The one tells its readers something they already know, tries to remove doubt about it, insists no further information is necessary. The other denies accepted knowledge, challenges an accepted belief-system, demands a story which shall explain how the picture and the belief-system can be made to relate.

From this sketchy example two points ought to emerge, both to science fiction's collective credit. One is about complexity of technique: a quality rarely praised in science fiction writers, who indeed often show great simplicity of technique in dealing with things in which they are not interested – character, for example, feeling, the fine social and moral discriminations which have been the staple of the English novel for centuries. Still, their compensation for this ought not to be entered solely on the side of 'ideas' or 'concepts', as so often it is. A good science-fiction story also often functions in an admirably Barthesian way, popping in and out of the 'turnstile' between myth and language, speaking now on the level of symbol and abstraction, but the next moment on the level of individuality and story, never allowing the reader to settle dully into either. The second point, more traditionally, is about the value of science fiction's subject matter. This claim too may seem incomprehensible to many doubtful or reluctant readers. Yet is is very easy to argue that people read and write science fiction in modern Western countries because it enables them to state and understand things about their own societies which verge on the taboo. The *Paris-Match* cover, as Barthes well saw, was making a statement of control and conformism. The *F&SF* one may have been elegiac rather than critical, but it was offering a national ideal something other than reverence: it was considering the notion that America might (would? should? must?) eventually fall.

Stories of 'the Fall of America' have indeed been common for a long time, and fit without much persuasion into several recognizable types. Especially popular after World War II was what one might call the 'survivor story', in which an individual or a group survived by cunning and violence in the ruins of a shattered America: classic examples include George Stewart's *Earth Abides* (1949), Wilson Tucker's *The Long Loud Silence* (1952) or Algis Budrys's *Some Will Not Die* (1961). A variant type is the 'America invaded' story, in which a small band of heroes throws off the shackles of the Pan-Asian/Soviet/alien invaders by using the traditional American strengths of technical ingenuity, freedom from superstition, irreverent humour, etc. This sub-genre was launched by Robert Heinlein's *The Day After Tomorrow* (original title *Sixth Column*, 1941) and continued in William Burkett's *Sleeping*

Planet (1964), Larry Niven and Jerry Pournelle's *Footfall* (1986), the recent video-film *Red Dawn*, and M. T. Engh's *A Wind from Bukhara* (original title *Arslan*, 1976), with a commendably and unusually thoughtful example in C. M. Kornbluth's *Christmas Eve* (original title *Not This August*, 1955). Yet in both 'survivor' and 'invasion' types, one should note that the Fall of America itself functions mainly as a datum, a way to get the real story started. Why the bombs should have been dropped, how the invasion could have been a success, are not questions generally posed. Concomitantly with this, American values are there to be revived or reasserted, not exposed to doubt.

Yet there are some stories, mostly from the seventies and eighties, which present a different scenario. In them the Fall of America is at least arguably America's own fault. The actual form of the Fall may involve occupation from outside or a kind of collapse under American society's own weight, but the most common element is neither war nor occupation but *domination*. The America presented in these stories is administered, or kept down, or financially overshadowed, by some foreign nation or nations: Arabs or Japanese, in stories discussed below; an international coalition in Kim Robinson's *The Wild Shore* (1984); an extra-national 'Peace Agency' in Vernor Vinge's *The Peace War* (1984), with responsibility piled elsewhere on Mexicans, Africans – almost everyone, in fact, except the Russians (too like the Americans to create an interesting situation) and the British (perhaps for reasons of historical sentiment). The roll-call of dominating powers in itself indicates the reasons for a loss of national morale: defeat in Vietnam, the Iranian hostage crisis, the oil crisis of 1974, the penetration of American markets by Japanese goods, all of which have shaken American self-belief in different ways. But what is interesting in the science-fictional reactions to recent history is the suggestion that not only American realities but also American values have been (will be, must be) in some way affected. Like the *F&SF* cover already discussed, this new sub-genre of 'Fallen American' stories exploits with particular force the techniques and ironies of 'disfigurement'.

Consider for instance a scene in Mike McQuay's novel *Jitterbug* (1984). It takes place at a sports field outside New Orleans, where the characters have gathered to watch 'our national pastime' – which turns out to be a game between gene-engineered humans, most of them wide, low, and weighing some 600 pounds, but others 15 feet tall and looking like 'walking toothpicks'. As one could guess from the physical types, the game played is a cross between two of the three distinctly American professional games, basketball and American football. But the 'ethnicity' of the scene is both rubbed in and rubbed out by the ceremony at the game start: 'A large holo of Faisel ibn Faisel Al Sa'ud appeared in the middle of the field, and the musak switched to the Arabian National Anthem, everyone in the bleachers standing and bowing his head.'

In at least four ways – not counting the game about to be played – this scene is as American as the Statue of Liberty. It has 'musak'; it has 'bleachers' (first recorded by the *OED* from New Haven in 1892); it has the playing of a national anthem, done at all professional games in the USA, but only at international level in the UK, and then greeted with general embarrassment at best; and it has the ritual of 'standing and bowing [one's] head'. This detail is admittedly not normal in the USA, where the rule is instead to stand at attention and (if the US flag is displayed) to place the right hand over the heart. But then McQuay's alteration of an established ritual contributes to the point being made in this scene of equal and opposite force to 'ethnicity' or 'Americanness', namely, defacement, insult, subjection. The American crowd is standing for the *Arabian* National Anthem; it is venerating a *person*, not an institution, and a foreign person at that; the crowd bows its collective head, to indicate not free allegiance but forced submission.

The submission is forced (we learn from the story) not only by economic considerations. What the oil producers have done is to install golden domes in all major world cities, ostensibly as advertising devices but in fact to contain and threaten the release of the herpes-based 'Jitterbug' virus, a mutated, incurable, contagious organism which creates in quick succession impotence and death. After the destruction of Australia and the USSR by the 'Jitterbug', the house of Sa'ud begins a two-century domination of the world, enforced by control over money, energy, and disease. America, clearly, can do nothing about this. McQuay's novel is in a way a 'scare' story, hinting not very darkly that all the above is only an extrapolation of the events of 1974; its moral lies in the threat that even the most distinctive Americanisms could be taken over without symbolic resistance. But there is an element of the wilful in the 'scare' that McQuay throws. In the end he is unable to accept the logic of his own position, allowing his central characters to repeat, *mutatis mutandis*, the ending of *Huckleberry Finn* and float off in a balloon to Wichita, where, they feel, there will be no dome and no 'Jitterbug'.

America, in that novel, accepts subjugation but does not actually commit self-betrayal. A further step in the direction of 'disfiguring' a national self-image is taken by Norman Spinrad's story 'A Thing of Beauty', from 1973.[5] This story consists of six scenes. In the first, an American called Harris is visited by a Mr Ito, of Ito Freight Boosters of Osaka, a 'typical heavyweight Japanese business-man' (Harris reflects), 'a prime example of the type that's pushed us out of the center of the international arena'. Harris, it transpires, makes his living by selling major Americana to foreign collectors. In the first scene his relationship with Ito wavers between superiority (for Ito's main motivation in seeking an American artefact is a wish to upstage his in-laws) and subservience (for Ito has both money and an Oriental tact over matters of 'face' which Harris cannot rise to). The next five scenes develop the contest between American and Japanese, over the sale of America.

What major artefact should Harris sell to Ito? Since the story is set in New York, the first thought must naturally be: the Statue of Liberty, known to Harris as 'the Headless Lady' – 'insurrectionists', we are told, blew its head off, though we are not told why. But Ito rejects his suggestion immediately. He agrees that the Statue is 'a symbol of America itself', but in its present state sees it as a reminder only of 'decline from your nation's past greatness'. To enshrine the Statue in Kyoto would be 'an ignoble act', a form of gloating. Harris does not share this feeling at all, regarding the Statue as 'just one more piece of junk left over from the glory days'; he loses face by being prepared to sell what Ito is not prepared to buy. But 'the customer is always right.' Harris's second attempt is to try to sell the Yankee Stadium, home of that third American professional game baseball, though the Stadium is now derelict and the game played apparently only in Japan. There is something both perceptive and imperceptive in this selection by Spinrad: perceptive in that American sports are so strikingly 'ethnic', being rarely or never played by outsiders; imperceptive in the assumption that in a non-American-dominated future, they might somehow have caught on. But in any case Ito declines to buy the Stadium. *He* would like to have it, but his in-laws regard baseball as totally uncultured, so it would bring him no prestige. Harris's third try is to attempt to sell Ito the UN Building: an artefact unlike the Statue of Liberty 'in excellent repair', apparently because the 'insurrectionists' who destroyed the one 'had had some crazy attachment' to the other. But this try gives serious offence. Ito has no respect for the UN or its Building at all; he feels neither nostalgia nor excitement; to him the building does not mark 'one of the noblest dreams of man' but only 'a shrill and contentious assembly of pauperized beggar-states united only in the dishonorable determination to extract international alms from more progressive, advanced, self-sustaining, and virtuous states, chief among them Japan'. At the end of this triad of symbolic scenes Harris has failed. He cannot think of anything American which would confer status on a Japanese.

Is this Harris's fault, or America's? The answer comes in the two last scenes. In the first, returning disconsolately to base, Mr Ito suddenly sees a 'magnificent structure' and demands to know if it is for sale: the structure, filthy, crumbling, disused, is Brooklyn Bridge. Now the main point about this in an American belief-system (as Harris immediately remembers) is that it is a joke. It is the thing traditionally sold by city con-men to 'suckers' from the sticks. For Mr Ito to want to buy it, then, makes him a 'sucker' and relates the whole story to the highly ethnic American proverb, 'Never give a sucker an even break.' When Harris says to Ito, 'I can think of no-one more worthy of that honor than your esteemed self, Mr Ito', the Oriental ceremony of his language conceals a much-relished insult. The contest between the two has been won by the American. Yet in the last scene his triumph is violently reversed. Harris, sitting in his office, receives a holo slide of Brooklyn Bridge, refurbished, in its new environment; it is, even he admits, 'very beautiful'. In an accompanying package from Ito there is a gold brick. Not a brick painted gold to sell to 'suckers', but a bar of real, pure, solid gold, crafted to look like a painted brick. Harris does not know what this means at the end, but we do. It means he was the sucker. He sold what he thought was a fake; but his customer knew it was real.

What this story very clearly means is that the Japanese is the true American. It is Ito who shows strong feelings about baseball, sadness over 'the Headless Lady'. He respects the icons of America as the American does not. As for his rejection of the UN Building, what this proves is: (a) true Americans, like Ito, do not respect the UN; (b) false Americans, like the 'insurrectionists' who spared the building and the federal authorities who keep it 'in excellent repair', do; (c) Harris has more in common with these latter groups than with Ito; they are all against America. Spinrad's fable is in fact interestingly balanced between a creditable openness – being American to him is not a matter of nationality – and a strongly chauvinist anger against Americans who betray their country and against an internationalism he finds incompatible with patriotism. There is a kind of symmetry, even, in the fate of the artefacts he mentions. Brooklyn Bridge can move to Osaka (where 'Americanism', we may conclude, is alive and well); but the Statue of Liberty, literally and symbolically 'disfigured', has to stay where it is. Yet both movement and stasis symbolize failure, a failure whose icon is 'the Headless Lady'.

The 'disfigurement' of the Statue of Liberty in 'A Thing of Beauty' is interestingly different from that of the *F&SF* cover. On one level (that of story), it is less. In Spinrad's world the history of the Statue has not been forgotten, is well-known, forms indeed part of Harris's sales-pitch. But on the level of myth the 'disfigurement' is much greater. The Statue has been decapitated, leaving it symbolically blind; it still holds a torch, but can no longer see its own light. Evidently, the Statue is America, showing a light to the rest of the world, unable to see that light itself, self-blinded (the 'insurrectionists' were Americans), self-mutilated. On another level, one could say that the Statue is like the gold bar which Harris, the slicker/sucker, thinks is a brick. What all this says is that Americans have betrayed/are betraying themselves – a theme repeated in Spinrad's interestingly parallel fable of an African-dominated future, 'The Lost Continent'.[6] Yet two things are missing from Spinrad's fables. One is any direct questioning of American ideals, as opposed to American realizations of those ideals. The other is any explanation as to how all this happened, how the Fall got started. Other science fiction writers, naturally, have tried to fill these gaps of history and of critique.

An interestingly if deliberately non-serious example is Frederik Pohl's story 'Criticality', from the *Analog* issue of December 1984.[7] This is set in New York, once again under foreign domination, indeed foreign occupation. This time the occupiers seem to be almost everyone: Canadians during the story's short time-span, but only as a relief from the Gurkhas, while independent nations operating within the USA include the Apache, Alaskans, and Puerto Ricans. Nobody in Pohl's world, it seems, wants to be an American at all – except the Americans. Yet the surprising thing about his story is that the only Americans we meet in it, Marian and the narrator, are perfectly happy with their situation. For most of the story, a Canadian member of the occupying forces is trying to persuade the narrator that he ought to take offence more readily, and to get Marian to accept his proposal of marriage. Neither American understands him. What holds them up is what lost America the war and what gives the story its title, a quality for which no one has yet found an accepted word. Briefly, it is (on a personal level) the habit of 'rating' people: seven for grooming and five for originality, eight for figure and six for perfume. On a social level it involves total tolerance: the narrator is unable to give the people who burgled his house anything but high marks for ingenuity. On a political level it seems to include both: Americans are very critical of their politicians, but also totally forgiving. The president who lost the war gets re-elected because, as the narrator says, 'he *acted* . . . he fired his Secretary of State and shook up the CIA. He acted fast and hard – what more could you ask?'

There is a good deal that is recognizable in Pohl's portrait – the omnipresent 'how did you rate our service?' forms in American hotels and diners, the sense that voters are playing a complex game with their politicians – but clearly Pohl is trying to identify a more general underlying cultural pattern (one, note, and see p. 108 above, never identified before). One could summarize by saying that in his view Americans (a) have lost/are losing the ability to tell right from wrong, seeing everything instead as complex shades of grey; (b) have done/are doing so because of seeing life as a spectator sport, or perhaps as a string of commercials. 'Criticality' flourishes in what another science fiction writer,

Kim Robinson, calls 'mallsprawl'. In the mall of life there is nothing to do but shop judiciously.

Pohl's fiction, symbol-free but jammed with detail, gives an answer on the level of story to the questions left aside by Spinrad's more evidently mythic fables: how will it happen? What's going wrong? Its jokiness may deter one from putting too much weight on it. Yet it is striking to see a kind of corroboration for it coming from Ursula Le Guin's story 'The New Atlantis' (1975),[8] a story which furthermore adds a new twist to the notion of 'disfigurement'. 'The New Atlantis', to be brief, appears to centre on the notion of American capitalism. And though it is extremely dangerous to venture on the notion of 'sources' in this fluid field, it does look as if 'The New Atlantis' is not only a conscious rejection of Francis Bacon's essay, but also of a nearer progenitor, Robert Heinlein's sexist, cliché-ridden, deeply reactionary but rather striking story 'Let There Be Light', from 1940.[9] What connects the two stories is that they are both about the notion of a 'sun-tap', an efficient form of converting solar power. The Heinlein story, however, exists to say that although American capitalism is dishonest – the 'sun-tap' is kept off the market by vested-interest utility companies – it still delivers the goods. The inventors solve their social problem (making a profit) by giving the invention away and then charging a tiny royalty on production. Capitalism means you can get rich and do good, says

Heinlein (though you must never do good for nothing, or expect others to take a loss on moral grounds). Le Guin parallels the Heinlein technology; definitely rejects his ideology; yet, oddly, places herself in the same doubtful world of capitalist apologia/critique.

At first glance, her world looks like a horrid extreme of American capitalism, a parody of all the things Heinlein so readily accepted. She has noted, for instance, the deep isolation of American sport, her heroine having to listen to a neighbour playing 'the weekly All-American Olympic Games at full blast every Sunday morning from his TV set'. More significantly, her world is drowned in advertising, everything over-promoted and under-fulfilled, so that a 'Supersonic Superscenic Deluxe Longdistance coal-burner' means a broken-down steam bus; the 'Longhorn Inch-Thick Steak House Dinerette' sells meatless hamburgers; the Supreme Court does commercials, and the universities 'don't teach much but Business Administration and Advertising and Media Skills any more'.

Yet a closer look leaves one much more uncertain. See, for instance, the following paragraph:

> I looked at the bottle. I had never seen aspirin before, only the Super-Buffered Pane-Gon and the Triple-Power N-L-G-Zic and the Extra-Strength Apansprin with the miracle ingredient more doctors recommend, which the fed-meds always give you prescriptions

> for, to be filled at your F[ederal] M[edical] A[uthority]-approved private-enterprise friendly drugstore at the low, low prices established by the Pure Food and Drug Administration in order to inspire competitive research.

What targets are being hit here? And how? The 'Super-Buffered Pane-Gon' is another perversion of capitalism; effort goes into slogans and sales, not product efficiency. The same joke underlies 'miracle ingredient more doctors recommend' and 'friendly drugstore', both well-established media phrases in reality. But what about the 'fed-meds' and the 'FMA'? How has government got mixed up with supporting private-industry products? More than supporting, prescribing? The public image of capitalism is that it works by competition, decisions being made by free purchasers. But clearly that is not the case with Le Guin's heroine, who has to take what is prescribed for her (unless she can get aspirin on the black market). The fed-meds prescribe commercial products; the patient has to fill them at a 'private-enterprise' drugstore, but one that is 'FMA-approved'; the price paid is established by government agency; but allegedly 'to inspire competitive research', presumably between private-company laboratories. It all sounds as if in 'The New Atlantis' the State has taken over, while still continuing to maintain a facade of respect for the free-market ideology. So is this maybe a *Communist* world? The trees in the 'National Forest Preserve' 'all had little signs on saying which union they had been planted by'. There are 'nasty rumors' about the Rehabilitation Camps and FMA Hospitals. The FBI arrests anyone with purple fingers on suspicion of circulating material via 'Sammy's dot' (ie *samizdat*). Somewhere in the background, a rebellion is going on by the Weathermen and 'Neo-Birchers'. Is this a left-wing view of dystopia or a right-wing one? Who can say? Does it matter?

To revert to Barthes, one can see that a phrase like 'Super-Buffered Pane-Gon' would be extraordinarily difficult to decode in terms of signs, signifiers, and signifieds, first-and second-order systems. It contains 'pain-killer' and 'hype', 'advertisement' and 'private enterprise', on linguistic and ideological levels, but also (from other elements in the paragraph) evident irony and ideological challenge. Probably no two critics would agree on which order these are perceived in, and if an order were agreed it would disappear again as soon as one tried to take in complications outside the phrase, outside the paragraph. Le Guin, one might say, moves round the Barthesian 'turnstile' of myth and language too quickly to be caught. But in any case a large part of her point is the total unreliability of the public language she uses, and of the myth it is designed to express. Overshadowing the whole story of the 'sun-tap' is the assertion that America is sinking (drowned symbolically by the heroine's tears). State reaction is to advertise real estate on land-fill and put up billboards with cute Disney-style beavers proclaiming 'IT'S NOT OUR FAULT!' Nothing, it seems, can get through the instant, skilled, verbalizing response, not even free energy and a cure to the State's problems. It does not matter whether the verbalizing is private-enterprise or public-administration. It is all a sequence of complex rhetorical 'figures' expressing an ideology to which only lip-service is paid. Le Guin does not have to decide, in a way, which ideology she is rejecting. In parodying public language, in 'dis-figuring' its 'figures', she is rejecting language, myth, and competing myths all at once. At the end, the story is presented as a message in a bottle, left to bob on the dark seas which will have covered/are covering the towers of New York: an image like the *Amazing Stories* cover of February 1964, of the Statue of Liberty buried shoulder-deep in cracked mud, observed by space-suited visitors from a flying saucer.

'The New Atlantis' is a confusing story (more so than has been indicated), with many targets including energy policy and sexual politics as well as creeping State control and public language. It is tempting indeed to take it as an overall and extreme *Verneinung*:[10] a collective 'No' to the whole American cultural mix, from commercials to divorce and the ethic of continuous sexual dynamism. It does raise the question of what residual loyalties are possible. To American rituals (McQuay)? Past American ideals (Spinrad)? Drowned American decencies (Le Guin)? Put another way, what deserves to be dug up out of the past? Yankee Stadium or the Statue of Liberty? Oddly but not altogether coincidentally, this issue is solved in similar form by two very recent 'novels of disinterment', which consider the question of what un-disfigured myths of America there may still be left.

These are Kim Robinson's *The Wild Shore* (1984) and David Brin's *The Postman* (1985). Both are 'post-Fall' novels, set on America's West Coast. Both take place 'after the Bomb', which in Brin's case generates a relatively traditional setting – 'Three-Year Winter', heavy 'die-back' among survivors, all leading to an America of small pre-feudal settlements. The collapse in Robinson's novel is more original: some foreign power (no one knows who) has driven two thousand neutron bombs into major cities, and set them all off as simultaneous car-bombs. But since then there has been a technological embargo on the USA conducted by the rest of the world. Japanese and Mexican ships patrol the California coast. Any attempt to build a railroad or restart unification draws laser fire from the sky. The world has concurred with the neutron bombers' judgement. Did America do this to itself, is Brin's question. Were they right to do it to us, is Robinson's.

The latter question centres in Robinson on Tom

Barnard, the mentor of the teenage gang whose fortunes *The Wild Shore* follows. Barnard is so odd as to be a curiosity, a figure close (for the teenagers) to myth. 'I am the last American,' he says,[11] and he teaches his pupils authoritatively about America. Yet much of what he says is false. He makes the narrator, Henry, learn chunks of poetry, but relates them instantly to his own childhood. As Henry recites the speech from *Richard II* – 'with eager feeding, food doth choke the feeder' – Barnard breaks in: 'That was us all right . . . He's writing about America there. We tried to eat the world and choked on it.' But when Henry reaches the John of Gaunt speech – 'This blessed plot, this earth, this realm, this England' – he breaks off. 'You can see why Shakespeare thought England was the best state,' says Henry. 'Yes,' says Barnard, 'he was a great American.' Like other paragraphs discussed above, this creates a strongly mixed effect. The boy Henry is totally misled. Why has Barnard misled him? To create nostalgic patriotism? If so, why the comment about 'tried to eat the world and choked on it'? We get a glimpse here of a kind of 'new text' Barnard is composing, a text in oral memory alone, a text which 'reads' Shakespeare as an American, and which assumes that America is the 'only begetter' of the past.

Yet every reader realizes this is a false text, and soon the teenagers do too. The first scenes of the book show the gang digging up a coffin – its headstone says '1919–1984' – because Barnard has told them the old Americans buried their dead in coffins with silver handles. But when they dig the coffin up, its handles are silver-coloured plastic. You got a poor man, says Barnard. They wouldn't have coloured the handles silver, argues one of the gang, if they hadn't been real silver once. At this point many readers ignorant of American funeral customs may be genuinely puzzled: is Barnard lying again? Is his image of the old America partly true, or all a pious fraud? The provocations within the text are frequent, and Barnard himself keeps changing his mind. America 'tried to eat the world,' he says. But when Henry challenges him for havng told them all their lives how great America was, he replies:

> 'America was huge, it was a giant. It swam through the seas eating up all the littler countries – drinking them up as it went along. We were eating up the world, boy, and that's why the world rose up and put an end to us. So I'm not contradicting myself. America was great like a whale – it was giant and majestic, but it stank and was a killer . . . Now haven't I always taught you that?'

'No,' says Henry. And still later, still protesting that 'America was evil,' Barnard insists: 'we didn't deserve it. *We were a good country*.'

The debate extends round and past Barnard as an

attempt is made to organize a Resistance against the Japanese. It's not worth it, says a gang member's father: there's no point in fighting 'for any idea like *America*'. He says this 'like the ugliest sort of curse', glaring at Barnard as he does so. But by contrast, when the boys do join the Resistance, a member comments, 'Good to know that someone in this valley is an American.' Most ambiguously, when Barnard and Henry go south to see the centre of Resistance, they find a white house erected incongruously on a piece of broken freeway over the flood-water, with above the house 'a little American flag snapping in the breeze'. At dusk the flag is lowered while everyone stands at attention. 'Tom and I stood with them,' says Henry, 'and I felt a peculiar glow flushing my face and the chinks of my spine.' Over-impressionable boy? Spontaneous patriot? No clear indication is given.

But this is not just a creditable even-handedness. This scene with the flood, the broken freeway, the white house, and the flag was in fact selected for the cover-illustration of the original Ace Special text; and one can see how close it is to the *F&SF* cover with which this essay began. We have a string of icons of America – including a white house like *the* White House – but they are 'disfigured' by water, disuse, ruin. Even the white house is made out of place, simply by being on a freeway. The reader is put in the position of someone in the past looking forward to a future where all we know has become blurred, fogged by degraded information, where our certainties can be achieved only by archaeological inquiry – when they will cease to be certainties and become matter for debate. The coffin being disinterred at the start is ours; the headstone date is that of the book's publication. One clear result of the whole process is that the sense which Barthes had of myth as undeniable – 'imperative', 'buttonholing', frozen, arbitrary, admitting none of the doubts and fullness of speech – this has vanished totally. No one can say for sure how to take the cover of *The Wild Shore*, or its scene with the flag, or the debate within it over America: 'disfiguring' myth returns it to the sphere of argument. Significantly, not only do the characters argue over Shakespeare, they argue also over the meaning of a picture: black sky, white ground, two white figures, a blue ball in the sky, and an American flag. Does this *prove* Americans went to the moon? We know it does. The characters do not. They have dug up too many fakes already.

Their story 'disfigures' our myths (see the cover), and for them our myths are 'disfigured' (see the moon picture), or perhaps rather 'defaced' – they have lost their value, like a defaced bank-note, or are suspected of being counterfeit. Yet one should note that in the 'white house' scene one item is *not* marked as out of place or inoperative, but remains doing exactly what it has always done and in exactly the same place as always: the American flag, snapping in the breeze. This last and undefaced icon of America survives in Robinson. It is foregrounded by David Brin.

His story also begins with a grave-robbing. Alone, stripped by bandits, close to freezing, his hero Gordon stumbles on a wrecked jeep. It is a US Postal Service vehicle with the skeleton of its murdered mailman inside. At first Gordon sees the mailbags and the mailman's jacket only as insulation; but on the jacket's shoulder patch is the American flag. When Gordon puts this on, he finds the scattered hill communities thrusting a role on him. He has to *become* the mailman, he has to deliver the letters, he begins to create new unity. He becomes the United States. The local tyrants, totally survival-orientated as they are, are afraid or ashamed to fire on the flag. Brin creates, in short, a neat argument about the nature of civilization: its essence is not freedom, or free enterprise, but sending letters and having them delivered – the existence, to put it more abstractly, of accepted channels of communication. Is that what the flag patch stands for? Is that the unity of the United States? A unity broken not even by the Civil War when, as Brin remarks, the US Mail continued to deliver letters across the battle lines for a full three years, as if refusing to recognize the conflict.

There is little doubt about the symbolism of the flag and the disinterred (or reborn) mailman in *The Postman*. Brin injects conflict into his novel by having unification challenged by a band of 'survivalists', who profess an extreme competitive-individualist code and insist that it represents the true America. But one could also, as a final twist, see the book as a conflict of texts:[12] the historical text of the survivalists, which proves (they claim) that *they* are the United States; Gordon's own journal, which proves all too clearly that he is a liar and there *is* no United States; the valueless, out-of-date, undeliverable letters for which men give their lives in the belief that *they* are the United States; one true letter which critically persuades a slave woman that Gordon's illusion of the United States is worth making the effort to realize. Perhaps the main point of Brin's fable of flags and texts is this. Everyone sees postmen every day; so often, in fact, that we have forgotten what they mean, or imply, or prove. We would understand this only if we did not have them. Then, indeed, they might become mythic figures, figures from 'before the Fall'. If the characteristic mode of science fiction is to take the Statue of Liberty and stamp 'CANCELLED' across it, Brin's mode is to take something never regarded as mythical and 'mythify' it.

Yet the operation in both cases is the same. One looks forward, to see people looking back. One takes present certainties, and views them through a haze of archaeological speculation. One takes arbitrary, frozen, inarguable myth, and surrounds it with enriching, explaining, confusing story. In their varying presentations of 'the Fall of America', science fiction writers show what they think of the icons of America now (and show that one of the meanings of America is freedom to do so). They also create artefacts which generate responses of extraordinary range and complexity. There is as yet no study of the tropes and techniques of science fiction; but it deploys an array of literary figures, especially in areas of doubt, limited certainty, and false comprehension for which we have indeed 'no name readily available among the familiar props of literary history'.[13]

NOTES

I would like to express my thanks to Krsto Mazuranic, of World SF, and to the British Council, for enabling me to give an early version of this paper at the 'World SF' Conference in Zagreb, Yugoslavia, in July 1986.

1 Cited here from Roland Barthes, *Mythologies*, selected and translated by Annette Lavers (London, 1973), but with reference to the original French text of 1957.
2 Ibid., p. 123.
3 The cover in fact illustrates Avram Davidson's story 'Bumberboom'.
4 The idea of 'disfigurement' is taken from Paul de Man's essay 'Shelley Disfigured', in his *Rhetoric of Romanticism* (New York, 1984), pp. 93–123.
5 First published in the *Analog* issue of January 1973, later reprinted in the Spinrad collections *No Direc-*

tion Home (1975) and *The Star-Spangled Future* (1979).

6 First published in the collection Anthony Cheetham (ed.), *Science against Man* (1970), but then reprinted in the collections in n. 5 above.

7 It should be said that Pohl has opened two recent novels with grim pictures of foreign domination, Arab-orientated in *The Coming of the Quantum Cats* (1986), Chinese-orientated in *Black Star Rising* (1985). Neither novel, however, maintains the story-line of its opening.

8 First printed in Robert Silverberg (ed.), *The New Atlantis and other Novellas of Science Fiction* (1975), but to be found also in Le Guin's collection *The Compass Rose* (1982).

9 First printed in *Super Science Stories* for May 1940, but most easily found in Heinlein's collection *The Man Who Sold the Moon* (1950).

10 The term is taken from de Man, 'Shelley Disfigured', p. 122. De Man here suggests, interestingly and perhaps for Le Guin appropriately, that *Verneinung* may indicate not only 'negation', but also 'an intended exorcism'.

11 Here he echoes a striking scene from Stewart's *Earth Abides* (1949), part II, ch. 5. Here, though, Ish is clearly a 'mythified' figure as Barnard is not.

12 De Man, 'Shelley disfigured', p. 95, asks: 'Is the status of a text like the status of a statue?' This would require a complex reply if one were to compare Brin and Spinrad, but it would be a revealing one.

13 Ibid., p. 98.

The Art of Future War: Starship Troopers, The Forever War *and Vietnam*

ALASDAIR SPARK

The science fiction author and critic Samuel Delany has argued that a defining characteristic of science fiction lies in the relationship between the empirical and the hypothetical, which he considers 'tri-valent' since

> The sf text speaks inward, of course, as do the texts of mundane fiction to create a subject (characters, plot, theme . . .) It also speaks outward, to create a world, a world in dialogue with the real. And, of course the real world speaks inward, to construct its dialogue with both.[1]

To this historian, what seems interesting about such trivalency is the referentiality between text and context; with this in mind, this essay will explore contextual and intertextual relations between two novels remarkable for their close links, Robert Heinlein's *Starship Troopers* (1959) and Joe Haldeman's *The Forever War* (1974).[2] The similarities (and therefore the differences) between the two novels are striking. Both won 'Hugo' awards from readers as best novel of their year (Haldeman also won a 'Nebula' from the Science Fiction Writers of America, a body not existing in 1960). Both are memoirs of war against an alien enemy far from home, giving space to combat, but also to training and civil-military relations, with many smaller parallels in situation, plot, and character. The key dissimilarity exists in attitudes towards the Army and military service, revealing the dominant bridge in real-time and fictional response of the Vietnam War. For while Heinlein's hero, Juan Rico, is proud to volunteer, in *The Forever War* William Mandella is conscripted – as was Haldeman in 1967.

Writing of *The Forever War*, Joe Haldeman (born in 1943) has admitted his debt to Heinlein:

> I got seventy pages into it before somebody pointed out that I had stolen the plot, all of the characters, all of the hardware from *Starship Troopers*. It hadn't occurred to me [but it] was my psychological background for the thing, and I subconsciously followed it.[3]

Consciously or subconsciously, science fiction has often involved writer replying to writer, developing and consolidating the genre. Tom Shippey has argued in his discussion of the heyday of science fiction magazines (1930–60), that this constituted a near 'collective mode' for readers, who 'simultaneously appreciated cross-reference, argument and parody in an almost subliminal way'.[4] Shippey's notion of a collective can be expanded to include authors, the vast majority of whom emerge from science fiction fans (including Haldeman) among whom this 'collective mode' survives today.

Of course, this is only part of the process of science fiction: outward referentialities are also vital, given that science fiction establishes its 'difference' in relation to the empirical present. In an essay written in 1959, the same year as *Starship Troopers,* Heinlein defined science fiction as 'realistic speculation about possible future events based solidly upon adequate knowledge of the real world, and on a thorough understanding of the nature and significance of the scientific method'.[5] But science fiction cannot be so utilitarian, since it inevitably falls victim to anachronism and obsolesence, and its real concern lies with a range of what 'might be'. Heinlein's own fiction fits ill with the above definition, since it is clear his concern is the construction of internally consistent extrapolation, establishing the coherence which, as Marc Angenot notes,[6] creates an 'absent paradigm' of the imagined world. Harry Harrison comments: 'You feel when you're reading [Heinlein] that when a detail comes in it's just one of a thousand details he could have included, not something he just invented on the spot, but part of a whole real world.'[7] But again, this is never neutrally arrived at: in science fiction the concerns of the present often manifest themselves in fear or expectation of the future, and from Verne and Wells onward, many works of science fiction have been written not to show what inevitably 'will be' or likely 'might be', but what 'ought to be' – or 'ought not'. By this didactic criterion, the genre provides not future history but present historiography, revealing of the presuppositions inherent in the speculation.

The science fiction of Robert Heinlein (1907–88) was clearly the product of a right-wing imagination. He began writing in the 1940s, having served in the US Navy until ill-health forced his retirement, and his fiction was seminal to the development of American science fiction. Critics agree on an engineer's concern for logic, and proficient, readable prose; equally they agree about Heinlein's near-unreadability at times,[8] because of the strident conservativism in such books as *Starship Troopers*. As Scholes and Rabkin note, Heinlein believes in life, liberty, and the pursuit of happiness for the individual;[9] equally, he has little faith in equality and fraternity for the collective, and denies the class struggle entirely. Generally, the trademark of all Heinlein's novels is a concern with citizenship and proper order, and Heinlein's opinions really belong to a 'native and proud of it' school epitomized by sceptical pundits such as H. L. Mencken, or the vulgar Nietzsche of Ayn Rand; he is perhaps best considered as a Social Darwinist, whose ideal society is one in which the individual is free to rise to his 'natural' level of power, wealth, and authority.

In the same 1959 essay, Heinlein ascribed to

science fiction the goal of 'preparing our youngsters to be mature citizens of the galaxy', and he wrote several juvenile novels such as *Starman Jones* (1953) where the concern is responsible adulthood, as Max Jones struggles to earn a place in the elite Guild of Astronauts. *Starship Troopers* was contracted as just such a juvenile novel by Scribner's in 1959; however, they refused to accept the manuscript, and the novel was published by Putnam's as adult science fiction.[10] The objections from Scribner's were presumably allied to those of many readers who found the novel distasteful, violent, and near-fascist. Put simply, it is the memoir of Juan Rico, a 'mobile infantryman' in a twenty-fourth-century interstellar war. The novel opens with an account of an assault on the home planet of the 'Skinnies', allies of the major enemy, the 'Bugs'. The story then flashes back to Rico's voluntary enlistment in the Army, despite his father's strong objections, and then an account of his harsh recruit training. Next follows a flashback within flashback to Rico's compulsory High School classes in 'History and Moral Philosophy' (H&MP), in which the central tenet of society – that military service alone earns the vote and full citizenship – is defended. The raid which begins the novel is returned to, and Rico's officer training follows, including H&MP classes. The novel closes with Lieutenant Rico commanding his unit on the eve of the attack on the Bug home planet, the Asiatically-named 'Klendathu.'

The novel was popular but, according to Sam

Lundwall,[11] reaction in the critical circles of science fiction was negative – one notable product being Harry Harrison's satire, *Bill the Galactic Hero* (1965). *Starship Troopers* also perhaps seemed an embarrassment to a genre striving for clean-living adulthood, and one is reminded of the outcry at the time against violent juvenile comic books. The 1967 NAL paperback edition (used for this essay) shows an embarrassed awareness of the novel's reputation, heightened by the fact of a real war in Vietnam. The blurb attempts to defuse criticism by describing the novel as 'appealing to those instincts (best kept suppressed) of violence and destruction' and proclaiming of the soldiers that 'neither the viciousness of their electronic armor, nor the bloodthirsty militarism of their training can save them from the grip of loneliness and fear.' Others have argued that the book is not to be taken seriously, and that Colonel Dubois, the History and Moral Philosophy instructor, is not Heinlein's mouthpiece – Haldeman believes Heinlein was not 'a hundred percent sympathetic' with the views expressed.[12] While one is reminded of Richard Usborne's comment on Dornford Yates, that it is difficult to tell whether his tongue is in his cheek or licking his lips,[13] evidence suggests that Heinlein wrote *Starship Troopers* as rather more than a juvenile potboiler. Revealingly, the novel is dedicated – itself unusual – to: '"Sarge", Arthur George Smith, Soldier, Citizen, Scientist, and to all

Starship Troopers, the Forever War, *Vietnam* sergeants anywhen, who have labored to make men out of boys'.

Critically *Starship Troopers* remains considered the juvenile 'militarist polemic' Alexei Panshin dubbed it in *Heinlein in Dimension* (1968),[14] being 'in no way an account of human problems or character development. There is no sustained human conflict. The story is the account of the making of a soldier . . . nothing more.' The stress laid on 'character development' and the like is redolent of college creative writing classes, and it does not strike Panshin that the novel might appear as personal and limited as memoirs written by veterans of World War I, World War II, and Korea. Heinlein was an aware, if limited, stylist, well able to satisfy Panshin's criteria, and some deliberation must be assumed in his efforts, since other features suggest *Starship Troopers* was not a hurried book. There are some notable and typically sly features which amount to more than the 'slick patness' Panshin accuses Heinlein of. One of the most interesting is Heinlein's use of structured absence – which Marc Angenot describes as when 'the sf narrative assumes a "not-said" that regulates the message. The rhetoric of credibility aims at having the reader believe not so much in what is literally said, as in what is assumed or presupposed.'[15] A simple but effective example is the transfer of locale from the North American standard to Latin America – the main character is called Juan Rico, and it is not New

York which is destroyed by the Bugs in their attack on Earth, but Buenos Aires. The same is true of race: Samuel Delany has recorded 'the shock of pleasure when halfway through the book the hero looks into the mirror and his black face looks back at him' – Delany being one of the few black science fiction authors.[16] A smaller gem comes in Rico's passing comment: 'I had some beautiful ear-clips . . . which had belonged to my mother's grandfather' (p. 144).

The violence in the novel perturbed readers, and certainly Heinlein's Mobile Infantry are murderous as, armed with everything from handguns to miniature atomic weapons, they raid Bug and Skinny bases and cities, aiming to inflict as much damage as possible – 'smash and destroy' Heinlein calls it, half-anticipating the war terminology to come. But what disturbed readers was perhaps not the killing, or even the scale of killing, for as Harry Harrison has pointed out 'military violence has been a stock in trade of science fiction since its inception.'[17] The upset is better traced to Heinlein's matter of fact tone of killing without regret, and refusal to censure his characters. Take a typical account by Rico:

> I didn't have time to fool with him; I was a good five hundred yards short of where I should have been by then. I still had the hand flamer in my left hand: I toasted him . . . A hand flamer is primarily for in-

> cendiary work, but it is a good anti-personnel weapon in tight quarters; you don't have to aim it much. (p. 16)

The objections can be imagined, yet this tone does resemble authentic memoirs of World War I and II. Compare this account by a World War II tank commander:

> We fired ... and sometimes that was enough to persuade the pillbox crew that the war held no future for them. But if not, we had a very effective weapon in one of the funnies ... which hurled a dustbin sized charge of high explosive. This usually succeeded in blasting the embrasure open and causing the occupants to lose all further interest in the campaign. Yet sometimes it didn't and then we carried out the third movement of the drill which was to bring up the flame-throwing tank ... There was no fourth movement ... it wasn't really necessary.[18]

Starship Troopers is intended to be a facsimile memoir, and in scenes of combat and training Heinlein strives for an authentic note – where the book starts to do the exact opposite for many readers is outside this orbit, in its moral and philosophical discussions.

One result is that military history peppers *Starship Troopers* – in service slang, names of ships, names of units, marching songs, anecdote, ritual, and in the moral instruction given to recruits. The same authenticity is given by quotations placed at the head of each chapter, drawn from the Koran, the Bible, Kipling, Churchill, and various military figures. Heinlein invents items of military equipment, ritual, and slang, but integrates them with tradition to complete the facsimile unit. Much of the character of the Mobile Infantry seems drawn from the US Marine Corps, though other distinctive flavours can be detected, such as the insistence that all recruits should speak in 'standard English', recalling the Foreign Legion (Sgt Zim, the drill instructor, seems as much a product of *Beau Geste* as *Sands of Iwo Jima)*, and the 'drops' onto the battlefield which echo elite paratroops. All this adds to the 'rhetoric of credibility', creating an apparent continuity with the 'past', in reality a dialogue with the present.

An apt characterization of combat and the military is important to Heinlein because *Starship Troopers* is fundamentally about relations between the soldier and the State, an issue current in the developing Cold War of the 1950s. For the best part of American history, there was agreement with what Niccolo Machiavelli wrote in *The Art of War* in 1521:

> There exists no more dangerous sort of infantry than one composed of men who make war their profession, since you are forced either to make war constantly

> and repeatedly pay these men, or run the risk that they will take your kingdom from you.[19]

Machiavelli pointed out the essential dilemma of civil-military relations: an Army and military expertise is required for the defence of the State, but also threatens the State, with the allied problem of choosing between unwelcome conscription or dangerous voluntarism to recruit troops. The traditional solution was to buy and pay off mercenaries, but to square the apparent made up only of citizens and volunteers. Civilian control of the Army in wartime would be assured, and in peacetime the Army would be largely disarmed, as the majority of soldiers returned home, leaving only a weak professional core.[20] This became the preferred model for America from the Continental Army onwards, and although conscription proved necessary in the Civil War and World War II, demobilization was mandatory. However, with the responsibilities of superpower status and competition with the Communist bloc, this proved inadequate, and intense discussion took place about whether the manpower required should be obtained via universal military service, volunteer-only service, or selective service, the latter being the eventual choice. Furthermore, as the military establishment grew during the Cold War, worries arose about the threat of military professionals, about America becoming a 'garrison state', and about the utility of armed forces in the atomic era.

Such military-political issues underlie *Starship Troopers*. In one of the compulsory History and Moral Philosophy (H&MP) classes which punctuate *Starship Troopers*, the instructor, Colonel Dubois, refers to 'the Mayer Report' (p. 157), one of several studies into the breakdown of morale and self-discipline among American soldiers in Korea, especially in captivity, where one in three GIs reportedly collaborated with the enemy. 'Brainwashing' was a popular explanation; another was suggested by Eugene Kinkead in his book *In Every War But One* (1959).[21] Kinkead's conclusion was that the failure was not just of 'our young soldiers who faced the antagonist [totalitarian communism], but more importantly of the entire cultural pattern which produced these young soldiers' (pp. 9–10). The concern was twofold: that the affluent society achieved by victory in World War II was not producing young men capable of service in the limited wars such as Korea which seemed likely to face America in the future; and that motivated soldiers should not lead to militarism that might threaten civil society. The solution, as Under-Secretary of the Army Hugh Milton suggested to Kinkead in 1957, was an American ideology as coherent and fundamental as Communism was imagined to be:

> The Army would like to see every American parent, every American teacher, and every American clergy-

> man work to instill in every one of our children a specific understanding of the differences between our way of life and the communist way of life ... By the time a young man enters the Army he should possess a sound set of moral values and the strength of character to live by them. Then, with Army training, he may become something very close to military perfection. The ideal citizen-soldier. (p. 211)

The Mobile Infantry are exactly such. As Rico says:

> In the past, armies have been known to fold up and quit because the men didn't know what they were fighting for, or why, and therefore lacked the will to fight. But the MI does not have that weakness. Each one of us was a volunteer to begin with. (p. 130)

The incentive (and soldiers can quit at any time) which Heinlein offers is citizenship, the central conceit of *Starship Troopers*, and the solution to the Machiavellian problem. The rationale is that

> since sovereign franchise is the ultimate in human authority, we insure that all who wield it accept the ultimate in social responsibility – we require each person who wishes to exert control over the state to wager his own life – and lose it if need be – to save the life of the state. (p. 156)

Hence, Heinlein's attention to recruit training at 'boot' camp, a harsh regime designed to 'run right out of the outfit those recruits who were too soft or too babyish ever to make mobile infantrymen' (p. 49). Several die in training, recalling the 1956 'Ribbon Creek massacre' in which six US Marines drowned during over-rigorous training.[22] The well-publicized scandal which followed forced the Marines to relax their practices, but Heinlein has no doubts: death is inevitable for soldiers; what matters is the nobility of doing it well, 'heads up, on the bounce, and still trying' (p. 53).

Heinlein takes Machiavelli to an extreme. Since the State wishes to provide soldiers, but at the same time to protect itself from them, Heinlein suggests the Army and the State should be a continuum – literally, citizen-soldiers. The result is a better Army, and a better society: there are no problems with soldiers since they are volunteers; no problems with citizens since they are proven responsible; and no problems with those who are neither, since they have not the mettle to cause problems – as Heinlein puts it: 'if you separate out the aggressive ones and make them the sheepdogs, the sheep will never give you trouble' (p. 156). Of course, contradictions abound: voting is not the same as governing, and if the State and the Military are reconciled by being the same thing, how can a democracy (even with a price of admission) operate and survive in an inherently hierarchical system based on obedience? What Heinlein is proposing here is actually a one-party state (ironically equivalent to totalitarian Communism), since all citizens are manufactured by the same process. The vote earned so harshly is in fact useless, except perhaps in status politics. The same point is evident in questioning how Heinlein's state might operate in peacetime: conveniently a war provides opportunities for service, but what is such a martial system to do in peacetime – except pick fights?

For all that, Heinlein's idea typically challenges by its apparent logic, and is not the product of a brainstorm. Much of the discussion – or rather the lecturing – given in the History and Moral Philosophy classes centres on the fundamentals of Heinlein's society, often via a review of the collapse of 'past' society – that is, our present. The pathology Heinlein 'recalls' is typical of that expressed in the late 1950s and early 1960s by conservative organizations such as the John Birch Society, and right-wing politicians such as Barry Goldwater, and it is not unreasonable to presume Heinlein was sincere.[23] He writes of the United States' collapse in 1987 – at the time the John Birch Society was predicting 1973. Colonel Dubois reflects on the break-up of the USA:

> Law-abiding people . . . hardly dared go into a public park at night. To do so was to risk attack by wolf-packs of children armed with chains, knives, home-made guns, bludgeons . . . Murder, drug addiction, larceny, assault, and vandalism were commonplace. Nor were parks the only places – these things

> happened also on the streets in daylight, on school grounds, even inside school buildings. (p. 99)

Conservative worries about child-rearing and Dr Spock, teenage rebellion and James Dean, motorbike gangs and Marlon Brando come to mind here; Dubois goes on to state that 'juvenile deliquency' is a contradiction in terms, being actually the result of inadequate punishment of the young:

> Were they scolded? Yes, often scathingly. Were their noses rubbed in it? Rarely . . . Were they spanked? Indeed not! Many had never been spanked even as small children; there was a widespread belief that spanking or any punishment involving pain did a child permanent psychic damage. (p. 100)

In Heinlein's fundamentalist society, parents 'paddle' their children, murderers are hanged, and public flogging is a standard punishment. Heinlein also hits out at standard figures in right-wing demonology such as the social workers and child psychologists he refers to as 'pre-scientific' and 'pseudo-professional' (p. 102). As for science, in an ironic echo of Marxism, Dubois celebrates the attainment of a 'scientifically verifiable theory of morals rooted in the individual's instinct to survive' which is now able to 'solve any moral problem on any level: Self-interest, love of family, duty to country, responsibility toward the human race . . .'

(p. 103). However, Heinlein dodges the exposition of such 'science': during a H&MP class Rico is told to 'bring to class tomorrow a proof in symbolic logic of your answer to my original question' (p. 152). Heinlein never demonstrates such proof himself – a structured absence indeed.

All the above is to verify the central truth taught by Heinlein, namely that Man has no instinct other than to survive and breed, and certainly no collective moral instinct. Competition is the basis of life, and 'the basis of all morality' 'is duty, a concept with the same relation to the group that self interest has to the individual' (p. 103). All that exists is the competitive instinct to survive and breed, which can be cultivated into morality if enforced by punishment. Therefore, military power and violence is crucially important to Heinlein, in the twenty-fourth or the twentieth century. Dubois tells his students:

> Anyone who clings to the historically untrue – and thoroughly immoral doctrine that 'violence never settles anything' I would advise to conjure up the ghosts of Napoleon Bonaparte and of the Duke of Wellington, and let them debate it. The ghost of Hitler could referee, and the jury might well be the Dodo, the Great Auk, and the Passenger Pigeon. Violence, naked force has settled more issues in human history than has any other factor, and the contrary opinion is wishful thinking at its worst. Breeds that

forget this basic truth have always paid for it with their lives and freedoms. (p. 27)

Even if human society becomes stable, the human race will inevitably fight with other 'breeds': 'Either we spread and wipe out the Bugs, or they spread and wipe us out – because both races are tough and smart and want the same real estate' (p. 159). No great leap is needed to see the comparison with Communism, and Heinlein's description of the Bugs fulfils the familiar 'yellow peril' stereotype of an Asian enemy, updated with Communist overtones during the Cold War. The Bugs, Heinlein writes, show as a collective hive species 'just how efficient a total communism can be when adapted to by evolution' (p. 131). The Bugs are caste-stratified (divided into Workers, Soldiers, Brains, and Royalty), inscrutable, and 'inhuman', chiefly in their willingness to spend lives. Rico says of the enemy (and note the term 'commissars'): 'the Bug commissars didn't care about expending soldiers any more than we cared about expending ammo. Perhaps we could have figured this out about the Bugs by noting the grief the Chinese hegemony gave the Russian-Anglo-American Alliance' (p. 131). Chinese human-wave attacks of the Korean War are clear in the above, another reference to the 'past', although Heinlein is canny enough to postulate a future Soviet-American alliance. The comparison of alien and Asian Communist is interesting, not least for the term 'Bugs' (the correct name would presumably be 'Klendathans'). This evokes the pejoratives applied to other Asian enemies such as Japanese, Koreans, and subsequently Vietnamese – people who, as GI memoirs repeatedly mention, were not considered human, but as mere 'gooks'.

Given a concern with violence, war as fought by the MI might seem absurd: a recruit asks about the need for infantry when H-bombs can destroy cities or whole planets at the push of a button. Sgt Zim replies:

> War is not violence and killing, pure and simple; war is *controlled* violence for a purpose. The purpose of war is to support your government's decisions by force. The purpose is never to kill your enemy just to be killing him ... but to make him do what you want him to do ... *We* supply the violence, other people – 'older and wiser heads' as they say – supply the control. (p. 56)

These were exactly the arguments used by the Army and Marine Corps to rebut claims that they were obsolete in the atomic age, and any reading of fifties strategic analysis by such as Thomas Schelling, Henry Kissinger, or Robert Osgood finds Heinlein's statement familiar within a rhetoric of limited war.[24] Ironically enough, such opinions were most often expressed by Democrats, and in this light, President Kennedy's inaugural promise to 'pay any price, bear any burden' and his demand of Americans that they 'ask not what your country can do for you, but what you can do for your country' takes on more than a tinge of Heinlein. Dale Carter makes precisely such a link between the American space programme of the early 1960s and the rhetoric of Kennedy's masculine promotion of the Astronaut Corps in a chapter in his book *The Final Frontier*, neatly titled 'Starship Troopers'.[25] Certainly, the parallel boosterism of the Green Berets (the Special Forces) reveals a desire for committed, motivated, volunteer citizen-soldiers, as resolved to win as Heinlein's troopers. Ultimately, *Starship Troopers* is a work of advocacy, suggesting that in a world of struggle civil-military relationships, attitudes to violence, and interventionism must alter. In the real world when they did, it led to Vietnam. When limited war was put into effect in the graduated bombing campaign and restrictions upon ground forces, the disputes between civilian and military authorities eventually led to a collapse of military strategy and civilian polity, something Heinlein's idealized civil-military continuum avoided, as neatly as it did the parallel collapse of morale among a drafted US Army.

Vietnam had considerable influence on American and European science fiction in the 1960s and 1970s, producing open debate in the letter columns of the magazines and, more covertly, in fiction such as Ursula Le Guin's *The Word for World is Forest* (1972)

Starship Troopers, the Forever War, *Vietnam* and other examinations of future colonialism. The most complete demarcation of opinion came with twin advertisements carried in *Galaxy* magazine in June 1968, listing authors for and against American involvement. In the Pro column was Robert Heinlein and much of the old guard of American science fiction. The Anti column contained a revealing box number in Milford, home of a new science fiction institution, the writer's workshop, and many signatories were identified with the 'New Wave' of 1960s science fiction. One reason the New Wave met with the success it did, particularly in Europe (the number of non-Americans being notable in the anti-war advertisement) in magazines such as *New Worlds*, lay with a diminishing faith in the promised all-American future, when confronted with present events in Vietnam. At the time of the *Galaxy* advertisments Joe Haldeman was in Vietnam, having been drafted into the Army after graduation in 1967. In September 1968 he was severely wounded by an explosion which killed several others, and was hospitalized until February 1969.[26]

In common with many veterans, Haldeman wanted to write about Vietnam, and the result was an autobiographical first novel *War Year.*[27] It was an unsatisfying experience, with the publisher insisting the novel be for juveniles, and *War Year* is hardly a good first novel. However, it is also worth noting that the Vietnam memoir is an inherently limited model, often offering only a replication of the impenetrable lack of meaning felt by soldiers in Vietnam, and giving little opportunity to discuss wider perspectives.[28] Recalling the origins of *The Forever War*, Haldeman said 'the only formal plan I had in mind ... was to address certain aspects of the Vietnam War in science fiction metaphor',[29] and he realized by 1971 that science fiction offered the means to make a statement which war novels – and publishers – forbade. That message was didactic: in 1977 Haldeman edited an anti-war science fiction anthology called *Study War No More* (1977) in which he wrote of his own wounding: 'you're thinking a lot of things, but one thing that doesn't cross your mind is that, as a student of war, you've flunked. You will never be objective about it, never again'[30]. It is both striking and appropriate that Haldeman's transferral of Vietnam to the future should essentially involve the re-telling of Heinlein's gung ho novel of a decade earlier.

The Forever War first saw publication in magazine form in 1972, and the stories were re-written for novel publication in 1974. *The Forever War* is a detailed novel, but in essence concerns the experiences of William Mandella (a partial anagram of Haldeman), drafted in 2007 with others from the elite of Earth to fight the 'Taurans', presumed responsible for the destruction of several starships. In 'Private Mandella', training takes place, and first combat on a 'portal planet' orbiting one of the black holes via which Mankind travels to the stars. 'Sergeant Mandella' concerns an abortive raid, the injury of Mandella's lover, Marygay Potter, in a shipboard accident, and their return to an Earth which has become unfamiliar, with the majority of the population homosexual. Both re-enlist and are badly injured in another raid; 'Lieutenant Mandella' concerns their convalescence together, and their eventual, and seemingly permanent, separation upon return to duty. 'Major Mandella' has Mandella training as an officer, and commanding his unit in the repulse of a Tauran attack on his base. Mandella and the survivors return home to find the war is over, having been revealed as due to a mistake.

As the above suggests, ironies are established and corrections made, but *The Forever War* is more than a rebuttal of Heinlein. As *Starship Troopers* was informed by the Cold War in its attitudes towards Communism, and its presentation of idealized military service, *The Forever War* is informed by an amalgamation of personal experience of Vietnam and reading of *Starship Troopers* to present a picture of what soldiers really get from service. By 1971, a decade of involvement in Vietnam had come to a close, and American troops were withdrawing in a difficult period for the morale of the Army. The Americans had 58,000 dead, 300,000 wounded; and a veteran population of some 2.9 million was coming to terms with the fact that America was not interested in their experiences, except perhaps to confirm a popular stereotype of the veteran as deranged by service in Vietnam.

Vietnam referentialities are immediately evident

in the 'Elite Conscription Act', suggesting a more repressive or more efficient draft, since as a college-educated draftee Haldeman was in a minority. The best do not have to volunteer, they are drafted, male and female alike, and whereas Heinlein's training is affirmative, Haldeman's contributes little. After a bridge-construction exercise Mandella muses:

> Here we were, fifty men and fifty women, with IQs over 150 and bodies of unusual health and strength, slogging elitely through the mud and slush of central Missouri, reflecting on the usefulness of our skill at building bridges on worlds where the only fluid is an occasional standing pool of liquid helium. (p. 8)

Twelve die in training, but unlike Heinlein with his bloodless, noble deaths, Haldeman shocks the reader with detail: 'There was a flash and a rumble and something hit her below the neck, and her headless body spun off end over end' (p. 23). Haldeman's soldiers do not go into combat with any confidence, and the slack morale of the US Army is extended into the future, as recruits answer back, freely smoke marijuana, and the required verbal salutation is 'Fuck You Sir!' – 'one of the Army's less inspired morale devices', writes Haldeman (p. 4).

Combat is bloody, and depicted with none of the matter-of-factness Heinlein employs. The most vivid descriptions Haldeman gives are of wounding, echoing Vietnam, not least his own injuries. When Mandella's lover Marygay Potter is hurt, Haldeman writes: 'She was still alive, her heart palpitating, but her blood-streaked head lolled limply, eyes rolled back to white slits, bubbles of red froth appearing and popping at the corner of her mouth each time she exhaled shallowly' (p. 87). Mandella discovers war means such power, 'I had a magic wand that I could point at life and make it a smoking piece of half-raw meat' (p. 48), but unlike Rico takes little pride in it. In fact, Haldeman's infantry do not fight very much. Unlike *Starship Troopers*, where combat involves attacks on Earth and the enemy's home planet, Haldeman's infantry fight far from home, raiding enemy bases on 'portal planets'. Far more time – in the order of months or years – is spent in transit or garrisoning bases, awaiting attack by the enemy. This strategic situation parallels Vietnam: the former resembles 'search and destroy' missions, the latter suggests the interminable firebase sieges of the war, as well as the perception held by GIs that they were bait for the enemy. The final combat in the novel (the attack on Mandella's command) follows what has become the paradigm of Vietnam combat fiction: a base is set up to bait the enemy; it is attacked, overrun, and hand-to-hand fighting ensues. Victory is won, but only by the destruction of the base (by 'nova' bomb in *The Forever War*, and napalm in, for instance, *Platoon*) suggesting the notorious phrase of the war, 'It became necessary to destroy the town in order to save it.'

As Haldeman presents them, military units are not bound together by pride, or even by the fact of fighting for planetary survival. In the central narrative device of the novel, relativity dictates that travel at the speed of light means that time slows down for those in transit, and while in life-time a few years have elapsed, back on Earth many decades have gone by – hence the forever war. The use Haldeman makes of such 'time-dilation' is discussed further below, but for soldiers it means that everything and everyone they might fight for is already lost. By the end of the novel Mandella finds himself in command of men and women whose language he cannot speak, whose sexual preferences he cannot understand, and who regard him as a perverse relic of the Dark Ages. This nicely exaggerates the generational gap between officers and enlisted men evident in Vietnam, and the effect of the US Army's rotation policy, by which each individual soldier served a one-year tour of duty in Vietnam, fragmenting cohesion.

As the direction of the novel suggests, the Taurans are not the Bugs – a name has been given to the enemy, but they are unknown. Mandella's first mission is to find a Tauran, and take it prisoner, but his unit first of all massacres an indigenous species by mistake – innocent civilians, in effect a moral echo of My Lai. When encountered, the

Taurans prove human in some features, and rather inept at combat. The slaughter that results is intensifed by post-hypnotic images implanted by the Army, depicting the enemy as Bug-like, and inducing a combat frenzy.

Haldeman resolves the Human–Tauran struggle in peace not victory, as the war is revealed to have begun 'on false pretences, and only continued because the two races were unable to communicate' (p. 232). The Tonkin Gulf incident and the revelations of the *Pentagon Papers* come to mind when Haldeman then attaches blame for starting the war to soldiers spoiling for a fight. Neither side has won, with Mandella's men the last to find out, as battle-scarred they arrive back at an HQ which 'exists only as a rendezvous point for returnees and as a monument to human stupidity. And shame' (p. 230). Peace has come because humanity has abandoned individuality in favour of a mass 'cloned' identity; since this is also the Tauran racial character, communication is possible and peace results. This precisely rebuts Heinlein, the implication being that two cloned, collective races will no longer compete, either as individuals, or as species. For all this, Haldeman's ending is unsatisfying, not least as the enemy are revealed to have been peace-loving, non-warriors all along. By providing a combat novel which finishes upon such a contrivance, perhaps what Haldeman really reveals is the common perception among Americans that the

Vietnam War was either a mistake or a fraud, but not really about anything at all, except perhaps American barbarity. But, as Heinlein at least is certain, war is always about something: in the case of Vietnam, a nation's future history. Whether one takes the side of the defeated South or the victorious North, the Vietnamese can hardly dismiss the war as a mistake or a fraud, not after thirty years of struggle and two million-plus casualties.

Perhaps the most effective use Haldeman makes of the Vietnam/future war model is in examination not of war but of veterans and problems of reintegration, a parallel made obvious by irony and exaggeration. Heinlein does not need to address this at all, since his veterans are central to society. Mandella's – and Haldeman's – experience is different. Because of time dilation, Mandella is trapped in a time machine – born in 1985, drafted in 2007, and surviving to the end of the war, he is then twenty-eight years old, while in historical time, 1,143 years have elapsed. Returning home to Earth with Marygay after his first tour, Mandella finds his brother is twice his age and lives on the Moon, his mother is in her eighties, and the world has changed radically. Neatly, it is apparently for the better; there is no poverty (in a nice touch, soldiers collect $400,000 in back-pay, but taxed at 98 per cent) and little crime, since everybody is conditioned to be happy. Equally, Mandella is welcomed home as a hero, but on the government's terms – when

Mandella and Marygay are interviewed on TV they find that their spoken doubts are edited out and replaced with warmongering (p. 121). Mandella cannot fit into his 'future'; qualified only for the military, he is unable to find work. He and Marygay finally re-enlist, on the promise that they will serve together as instructors, but both are too experienced not to be put in command. They are separated, a separation which seems permanent, since apart they will 'age' at different rates.

The feature of the future Haldeman uses most to express Mandella's alienation is gender. The future Mandella 'visits' becomes progressively homosexual, with heterosexual sex classed as a dysfunction. Haldeman's characterization of this is weak at times: men mince about, wear cosmetics, and are rather fey, while women are butch and aggressive, but this does serve to erode the familiar masculinist soldier identity – Mandella ends up in command of an entirely homosexual unit who nickname him 'the old queer'. The homosexual context serves to heighten the relationship and separation of Marygay and Mandella which forms the sub-text of the novel. In contrast, Heinlein deals with sex in the oblique manner of 1950s science fiction; but, although women are decorative as in Haldeman, they are also members of the military, and superior in some roles, as befits Heinlein's competitive society. The comparable sub-text of *Starship Troopers* is the separation between Rico and his father, reconciled when father joins up after mother is killed by the Bugs. At the end of *The Forever War*, Mandella and Marygay are reunited, as he finds she has waited for him, travelling back and forth at light speed ever since her demobilization, so that one personal month passes every ten years. Mary Gay Potter was the maiden name of Haldeman's wife, and the real message of *The Forever War* (the opposite of *Starship Troopers*) might be said to be an appropriate 'Make love, not war'.

To conclude, the intertextual links between *The Forever War* and *Starship Troopers* are remarkable, such that they might be described as two versions of the same tale. This linkage is revealing both of the process of writing science fiction, and of its essential referentiality to the empirical world, as the re-telling, modulated by national and personal experience of Vietnam, provided for Haldeman a means of expression which conventional fiction could not. As Vietnam recedes into memory the relationship between the two novels is still evolving, and revealing of the ironies of history. Heinlein's message that a committed Army backed by a committed society is needed to win a war was surely confirmed by Vietnam, but now that as a result the United States has a volunteer military, few feel greatly confident of its effectiveness. Haldeman's depiction has perhaps been redeemed by an increasing recovery of respect for Vietnam veterans, but recent events in Iran and the Lebanon

Starship Troopers, the Forever War, *Vietnam* show the impotence of military power against enemies who are the product of a truly fundamentalist society, and would seem to undercut any message of love.

NOTES

1 Samuel Delany, *The American Shore* (Elizabethtown, NY, 1978), quoted in Patrick Parrinder, *Science Fiction: Its Criticism and Teaching* (London, 1971), p. 112.
2 Robert Heinlein, *Starship Troopers* (1959). Page references are to the New American Library reprint, New York, 1967. Joe Haldeman, *The Forever War* (1974). Page references are to the UK reprint by Orbit, London, 1976.
3 Joe Haldeman (ed.), *Body Armor 2000* (1986), p. 4.
4 Tom Shippey, 'The Cold War in Science Fiction, 1940–60' in Patrick Parrinder (ed.), *Science Fiction: A Critical Guide* (London, 1979), p. 91.
5 Quoted in Parrinder, *Science Fiction: Its Criticism and Teaching*, p. 16.
6 Quoted in Darko Suvin, *Positions and Presuppositions in Science Fiction* (London, 1988), pp. 66–7.
7 Quoted in John Brosnan, *Future Tense* (New York, 1978), p. 281.
8 See for instance comments in Parrinder, *Science Fiction: Its Criticism and Teaching*; Robert Scholes and Eric Rabkin, *Science Fiction: History, Science, Fiction* (London, 1977); Alexei Panshin, *Heinlein in Dimension* (Chicago, 1968).

9 Scholes and Rabkin, *Science Fiction*, pp. 56–7.
10 Panshin, *Heinlein*, pp. 94–8. See also H. Bruce Franklin, *Robert Heinlein: America as Science Fiction* (New York, 1980).
11 Sam Lundwall, *Science Fiction: What's It All About?* (New York, 1971), pp. 67–8.
12 Quoted in Joan Gordon, *Joe Haldeman: Starmont Reader's Guide* (Seattle, 1980), p. 33.
13 Richard Usborne, *Clubland Heroes* (London, 1978), p. 27.
14 Panshin, *Heinlein*, p. 95.
15 Quoted in Parrinder, *Science Fiction: Its Criticism and Teaching*, p. 114.
16 Scholes and Rabkin, *Science Fiction*, p. 188.
17 Quoted in Brian Ash (ed.), *The Visual Encyclopaedia of Science Fiction* (London, 1977), p. 100.
18 Quoted in John Ellis, *The Sharp End of War* (London, 1982), p. 157.
19 Niccolo Machiavelli, *The Art of War*, extracts in Peter Bondella and Mark Musa, *The Portable Machiavelli* (Harmondsworth, 1979), p. 495.
20 Bondella and Musa, *Portable Machiarelli*, pp. 498–507.
21 Eugene Kinkead, *In Every War But One* (New York, 1959).
22 For details see J. Robert Moskin, *The Story of the US Marine Corps* (New York, 1979), pp. 596–7.
23 See Alan F. Westin, 'The John Birch Society', in Daniel Bell (ed.), *The Radical Right* (New York, 2nd edn, 1962), pp. 201–27. The other essays in this text are also useful.
24 Thomas Schelling, *Arms and Influence* (New Haven,

1966); Henry Kissinger, *Nuclear Weapons and Foreign Policy* (New York, 1957); Robert Osgood, *Limited War* (Chicago, 1957).

25 Dale Carter, *The Final Frontier: The Rise and Fall of the American Rocket State* (London, 1988), ch. 4, pp. 153–96.

26 Gordon, *Haldeman*, pp. 15–16. For an account of his service and injury see also Haldeman's introduction to *Study War No More* (New York, 1977).

27 Joe Haldeman, *War Year* (New York, 1972; rev. paperback repr. New York, 1978). See also Gordon, *Haldeman*, pp. 20–4.

28 For a discussion of Vietnam fiction, see for instance Thomas Myers, *Walking Point* (Oxford, 1989).

29 Haldeman, *Body Armor 2000*, p. 4.

30 Haldeman, *Study War No More*, p. 4. See also Joe Haldeman's editorial 'Sf and War', *Isaac Asimov's Science Fiction Magazine*, April 1986, pp. 3–7.

Origins of the Underpeople: Cats, Kuomintang and Cordwainer Smith

Paul Myron Anthony Linebarger was an American political scientist who specialized in twentieth-century Chinese history and government. He wrote the first comprehensive military textbook on psychological warfare. He also wrote two controversial mainstream novels, plus a spy thriller whose protagonist single-handedly destroyed a Soviet nuclear bomb factory several years before James Bond saw the light of day. Yet it was not until the last decade of his life, after he had achieved distinction in these other areas, that Linebarger found his true *métier:* as an innovative and influential science fiction writer, under the pseudonym of Cordwainer Smith.

From 1950 to 1966, Linebarger as Smith produced some of the most complex and powerful works in the genre. Most of the Cordwainer Smith stories were set within the framework of an elaborate 'future history', more romantic and mythic than Robert Heinlein's hard-edged future, more concerned with the moral development of humanity than Isaac Asimov's Roman Empire-inspired 'Foundation' series. Central to Smith's future history were the *underpeople*, creatures whose genetic origin was non-human but who had been artificially shaped to look and function like human beings.

Twenty years before he produced any underpeople stories, Paul Linebarger wrote in his personal notebook:

> Is it not likely, since so many generations of cats and dogs occupy but the lifetime of a single man, and since these beasts are subjected by man to a selective breeding not likely to apply in his own case for a very long time, that domestic animals will begin to talk in the next twenty or thirty thousand years? What will the order of their minds be? At first, of course, they will speak of concrete things, but later——
>
> Imagine the awe and dismay of the first man to whom the question is put, 'Why am I a cat?'[1]

Super-intelligent cats populated Paul Linebarger's fictional worlds even before he acquired the pseudonym of Cordwainer Smith.[2] Other essential elements of his science fiction may be found as early as the first Cordwainer Smith story 'Scanners Live in Vain' (1950): strange survivals from various eras of post-nuclear-holocaust civilization; humans physically altered to withstand the rigours of space travel; the time- and space-spanning government known as the Instrumentality of Mankind. But the underpeople did not begin to develop until his career as Cordwainer Smith was half over, and he completed every major underpeople story during a three-year period (1961–3). Why did the underpeople emerge at this time, and what was their significance for their creator?

In today's world of recombinant gene products and of monkeys trained as 'companion animals' for the physically handicapped, the basic concept of the underpeople may appear almost commonplace. But Linebarger's development of the concept gave it a depth and a resonance rare in science fiction. He used it to express the essence of his most deeply held political convictions, as well as to explore powerful psychological conflicts and difficult aspects of his complex life history. Thus an examination of the underpeople can tell us a good deal about the character of Linebarger himself, as well as about the development of his small but significant body of science-fictional work.

THE UNDERPEOPLE DEFINED

Linebarger distinguished clearly between underpeople (also called homunculi) and other creatures in his fiction. The Partners of 'The Game of Rat and Dragon' (1955) are cats – especially chosen for their telepathic abilities, but otherwise 'the same cute little animals that people had used as pets for thousands of years back on Earth' (p. 76). The

Beasts of several early post-atomic-war stories are animals who have retained their animal form, but who in certain instances can communicate with humans and have acquired such human habits as wearing glasses.[3] Hominids or 'trumen' are genetic human beings, whose external form may have been significantly modified for survival on other planets but who nonetheless remain legally human. In contrast to all these categories, the underpeople are neither animal in form nor human in origin, as Linebarger stressed in an early note to himself: 'There is, however, a very sharp line drawn between trumen and underpeople. Underpeople are adapted earth animals who are confined very rigidly to earth save for one or two infested planets where they are left relatively much in peace.'[4] The distinction is made even clearer in one of the first completed stories dealing with underpeople, 'Alpha Ralpha Boulevard' (1961):

> There were few hominids around these days, men from the stars who (though of true human stock) had been changed to fit the conditions of a thousand worlds. The homunculi were morally repulsive [to the human narrator], though many of them looked like very handsome people; bred from animals into the shape of men, they took over the tedious chores of working with machines where no real man would wish to go. [p. 287]

Origins of the Underpeople

The homunculi or underpeople are derived from cats, turtles, eagles, and other animal species, retaining not only the underlying genetic structure but the broad behavioural tendencies of their kind. They not only do the dirty work of a technological civilization, but function as 'girlygirls' (geisha-like hostesses), medical orderlies, and other kinds of menial workers. For several thousand years their legal rights have remained minimal; humans can severely punish or kill them for minor infractions. Then they begin to develop their own secret government, their own moral and religious aims, in direct though concealed competition with the largely amoral and areligious Instrumentality of Mankind. It is at this point that the underpeople become important to the Cordwainer Smith future history. Indeed, it is only then that they begin to be mentioned at all.

LITERARY ORIGINS

The literary sources of the underpeople are reasonably clear. Of the many writers in several languages whose fiction Paul Linebarger read as a youth, his favourite was H.G. Wells.[5] Among Wells's novels, *The Island of Dr Moreau* (1896) seems to have affected Linebarger especially strongly. As J. J. Pierce notes,[6] the ritualized Code of the Scanners in 'Scanners Live in Vain' (pp. 14–17) is based directly on the 'Are we not men?' chant of the Beast People in *Moreau* (ch. 12). Wells's chanting Beast People 'were not men, had never been men. They were animals – humanized animals – triumphs of vivisection.'[7] Cordwainer Smith's underpeople are, by and large, bred to look human rather than cut to look human,[8] but like Wells's Beast People, they are still animals beneath their human surface. Further, the one Beast Person to whom Wells gave a name, M'ling, apparently inspired Linebarger to name many of his underpeople with a capital initial followed by an apostrophe and a sequence of lower-case letters. (For the underpeople but not for M'ling, the initial letter denotes their animal origin: C for cat, D for dog, etc.) A final similarity is that Wells's Beast People also revolt against their masters, though much more violently than Linebarger's eventually spiritualized underpeople.

Other literary influences are likely, though less obvious. The Morlocks of Wells's *Time Machine* (1895), though not beast-derived, resemble the underpeople in their social functions, their underground habitat, and their conflict with the surface-dwellers. (The underground workers of Fritz Lang's film *Metropolis* display similar qualities and may have been partly inspired by Wells. Linebarger saw the film in 1927, about six months after he read *The Time Machine*.) Linebarger was also familiar with the work of Karel Capek, whose *War with the Newts* (1936) depicted vaguely human-appearing lizards who were trained to do lowly work for humans, then revolted against them.

Olaf Stapledon was another writer of literary science fiction whose work Linebarger strongly admired. Stapledon's novel about a highly intelligent talking dog, *Sirius* (1944), appeared only four years after Linebarger had speculated in his private notebook about the future development of talking animals.[9] Linebarger also read pulp science fiction, so a 1946 story by Edmond Hamilton, 'Day of Judgment,' may have made its contribution to the underpeople as well.[10] It depicts humanoid creatures developed from dogs, cats, and other animals after a nuclear war has destroyed nearly all life on earth. Upon discovering the last surviving humans, the animal-people first want to kill them but then work out a *modus vivendi* with them. The story is less sophisticated than Linebarger's work, but its similarities to his underpeople stories and to Wells's novel of the Beast People extend to the format of the principal cat-person's name, S'San.

POLITICAL AND HISTORICAL ORIGINS

Although these literary antecedents probably helped to shape Paul Linebarger's thinking, there is no evidence that they were immediately responsible for the birth of the underpeople. Linebarger read a great deal of science fiction (as well as other forms of literature) from an early age, and he could have chosen to develop further any number of established themes or literary constructs. The timing of his development of the underpeople, beginning on paper around 1958 and reaching its height in the early 1960s, remains to be explained, along with the strong moral and religious components of the theme, not notable in any of the obvious literary models.

Previous commentators have identified the underpeople as a device for representing American racial conflict.[11] The year 1958 occurred in the middle of a period that journalists have termed a 'revolutionary decade' in American race relations, beginning with the Supreme Court's school desegregation decision in 1954 and culminating in the Civil Rights Act of 1964.[12] Paul Linebarger, a political moderate on many domestic issues though usually rather conservative in foreign policy, was surely aware of widespread discrimination against blacks in America and of the swelling civil rights struggle. His expression of deep friendship toward his black housemaid, in an emotional book dedication after her sudden death in 1964 (*Space Lords* (1965), p. 5), has led some readers to assume that he was strongly committed to the cause of racial equality and that his introduction of the underpeople into his fiction expressed this commitment.

Arthur Burns, an Australian political scientist

with whom Linebarger became friends late in life, has put this sort of argument most bluntly: 'In his stories about the Instrumentality ... the underpeople keep on coming out – these animals which have been made over into human beings. Now this is a sort of social allegory for the American Negro.'[13] Burns's interviewer has expanded upon the same argument: 'In "The Dead Lady of Clown Town", "The Ballad of Lost C'mell", and "A Planet Named Shayol", to choose only three stories ... [Linebarger] writes strongly and with great feeling of the racial problems which surrounded him in his own land.'[14]

Other critics have responded similarly. 'The parallels with contemporary and historical racialist attitudes are obvious,' according to Terry Dowling.[15] Gary K. Wolfe elaborates upon those parallels:

> The growing sterility and excessive standardization of life during the Instrumentality's decadent phase suggests the leisure society that began to develop in the United States after World War II, and the systematic oppression of the underpeople suggests the racism which permeated that society.[16]

A remark by Linebarger's widow, in reference to their black maid Eleanor, seems to support the argument: 'There was sort of a personal feeling in the Negro parallel [with the underpeople] ... She

[Eleanor] really was like one of the family. Paul would get involved in a social issue only if it were first a personal issue. It was not out of idealism—there had to be something to trigger it.'[17]

However, Genevieve Linebarger was neither consistently well-informed about her husband's literary inspirations nor consistently accurate in her recollections. Her interviewer, J. J. Pierce, has expressed his own reservations about so simple a view of Linebarger's concept of the underpeople:

> Most critics tend to assume he intended it only as a metaphorical idea in connection with the American racial situation – and certainly the underpeople face problems similar to those of contemporary blacks. But similarity is not identity . . . the societies and cultures of true men and underpeople which clash in his future history bear hardly any resemblance to those of whites and blacks today, save for the existence of group prejudice (pp. 21–2).

Evidence exists that the American racial situation was not uppermost, nor even very high, in Linebarger's thinking during that 'revolutionary decade' when the underpeople took form. Linebarger was indeed firmly supportive of racial equality. He wrote proudly of the record of his academic institution, the Johns Hopkins University's School of Advanced International Studies (SAIS) in Washington, DC: 'On race, the school has never been segregated on any grounds whatsoever. It was chartered as a nonsegregated school and its dormitories and dining facilities have been open to persons without respect to race, religion, or previous condition of servitude.'[18] However, at the height of the Southern black revolution and in the same year as the publication of the first underpeople stories, Linebarger also wrote:

> the American people have behaved splendidly, the less educated often wiser than the educated in their acceptance of a harsh and changing world. All the races in the United States (white, Negro, Amerind, nisei, or wahkiu) have contributed; only the minorities of the minorities have made trouble and even in the face of war, taxation, depression, and racial irritation the minorities of all races have kept their temper.[19]

This is certainly a generous statement with regard to 'all races', and as a semi-official statement on behalf of SAIS it may be more diplomatically phrased than Linebarger personally felt. But it is not the statement of a man passionately involved in contemporary American racial issues or drawing powerful fictional inspiration directly from them. I have been unable to find any contrasting evidence that would imply a stronger involvement by Linebarger in mid-twentieth-century American racial controversy than this statement suggests.[20]

Nonetheless the emergence of the underpeople in

1958, as well as Linebarger's intensification of their struggle for equality simultaneously with the growing struggle of American blacks, probably involved more than coincidence. Rather than directly inspiring Linebarger's fiction or newly arousing his interest in racial equality, the black American struggle seems to have heightened the salience of his longstanding concern with such issues in a different milieu. Paul Linebarger had been intensely involved with the cause of ethnic underdogs for many years, beginning much earlier than the American 'revolutionary decade' of 1954–64. Indeed he had literally grown up identifying deeply with the fate of a vast body of underpeople: the common people of China.

At first he heard about these underpeople from his father. Seven years before Paul M. A. Linebarger's birth, Judge Paul M. W. Linebarger had decided to commit his life totally to helping Sun Yat-sen free the Chinese people from the tyrannical rule of the Manchu Dynasty.[21] The Manchus had entered China nearly three centuries earlier as alien invaders of a different racial stock. They had then deliberately introduced racial discrimination into Chinese government; as the ruling class, they exercised discriminatory powers ranging from mild to despotic over the native Chinese.[22] Judge Linebarger's conversion to Sun Yat-sen's cause was inspired by the testimony of a former servant who had been mutilated and tortured nearly to death by the

Manchus. The younger Paul visited China for the first time at the age of six; over the next decade he spent most of his intermittent Chinese stays in the protected foreign enclaves of Shanghai. But his father and other revolutionaries told him a great deal about the suffering populace and their brutal masters. The Judge was as harsh in his judgements of the British and other white powers in China as he was of the Manchu despots.

With its foundations laid by his childhood indoctrination, the younger Paul Linebarger's personal awakening to the plight of the Chinese masses came when his family returned to China in 1930, after three comfortable years in the United States. Instead of settling again in Shanghai, the family went to Nanking, where the sixteen-year-old Paul observed

> many disquieting things. I beheld vast masses of men in the bondage of pain. I experienced wild hatreds and sympathies that destroyed my detachment and egotism and set my brain on fire. I was nauseated in making my first acquaintance with violent death. I had but to look out of my window to see people beyond the walls of the mansion starving to death in mud huts. Everywhere I went I encountered misery . . . Though later the unpleasantness passed, though I grew more accustomedly callous to the human suffering about me, none the less the memory of the moods rather than the thoughts haunted me.[23]

Paul Linebarger's description of this experience is remarkably similar to young leftist activists' reports of the experiences that awakened them to the racial inequalities of America in the 1960s.[24] In Linebarger's case, the experience stimulated him to write a lengthy set of philosophical statements, to plan a grand (if not grandiose) cycle of fictional works dealing with Chinese history and his own life, and perhaps to sympathize temporarily with the Communist rather than the Nationalist side of Chinese politics. (Linebarger's widow told J. J. Pierce that he had developed 'radical leanings' at about this time, and that his father responded by giving him an eighteenth-birthday trip to Russia, which 'sufficed to cure the son of his sympathies for Communism'.[25]) Linebarger's later support for the Nationalist Government of Chiang Kai-shek, based as much on family tradition as on his personal relationships with Chiang and other government officials, was tempered by his knowledge of official corruption and incompetence. But Linebarger's sympathies for the Chinese people, whether they lived on the mainland, on Taiwan, or in various overseas locations, never wavered. It is these sympathies, more than any other, that appear to be expressed in the sufferings and aspirations of the underpeople.

Paul Linebarger remained politically a divided man, as his father had been before him. Judge Linebarger had built up a solid reputation as a lawyer, politician, and judge, only to abandon much of his political respectability when he joined Sun Yat-sen's revolutionary forces. He did, however, attempt to maintain some surface respectability, better to aid the revolutionary cause, but also perhaps to satisfy certain of his own psychological needs. The Judge's son Paul felt himself very much a part of the revolutionary movement as a child – as early as five asking the Judge, 'How do you play the game of the re-vo-lu-tion-aree?'[26] By the time the younger Linebarger embarked upon his own career as a political scientist, supporting the Nationalist Chinese Government was thoroughly respectable in the US and in time even became a conservative position. Paul Linebarger enjoyed his establishment connections in America and China. He talked the language of *realpolitik* with ease. As a member of Army Intelligence, he developed views about psychological warfare and political assassination that would hardly have disturbed his counterparts in the CIA. But like his father, Linebarger retained a deeply empathic feeling for the plight of the politically oppressed. Late in life he was unable fully to express those feelings within the context of his political connections, his academic reputation, and his family ties to what was by now an ageing and superseded revolution. Instead his love and hope for the Chinese masses came to be embodied in his vision of the underpeople.

Specific aspects of Linebarger's career as a political scientist may have encouraged that shift into fiction. In the mid-1950s he devoted a great deal of effort and travel to a study of the overseas Chinese – those living elsewhere than mainland China or Taiwan – and their attitudes toward the Kuomintang, the Nationalist Party of Chiang Kai-shek. Linebarger found the overseas Chinese, through adaptation to local circumstances, to have become unexpectedly diverse in their views. Some were even more conservative politically than those remaining on Taiwan; others were again becoming revolutionary in their aspirations. Linebarger discussed his findings in a scholarly book manuscript that he hoped would restore his academic reputation as a China expert – a reputation that had somewhat faded during his military work on psychological warfare. Several university presses rejected the manuscript, mainly (in Linebarger's opinion) for political reasons. He rewrote the manuscript, but after two years of negotiations with his own university's press, he received a final rejection on 12 February 1958.[27] Only three months passed before Cordwainer Smith's fictional drafts recorded the birth of the underpeople. As they grew, the underpeople displayed more than a few traces of the overseas Chinese and their politically oppressed kinspeople on the mainland.

PERSONAL ORIGINS

Literature, politics, and personal experience were always so closely intertwined for Paul Linebarger as to be inseparable. However, several factors in the development of the underpeople may be described as more personal than literary or political. Among them, Linebarger's concerns about religion, about death, and about intimate emotional relationships appear to have been especially significant in determining the forms taken by the underpeople and the dates of their emergence.

Paul Linebarger is often assumed to have been a committed Christian all his life, and to have expressed that commitment consistently throughout his science fiction. Several critical and biographical sources refer to his having had a 'High-Church Episcopalian' upbringing,[28] or to his being a 'High-Church Anglican,'[29] as if he had always been one. In fact the family tradition was decidedly Low-Church Methodist. Paul's paternal grandfather was a circuit-riding Methodist preacher; Judge Linebarger initially trained for the Methodist ministry; and Paul listed himself as a Methodist as late as the 1954–5 edition of *Who's Who in America*. However, the Judge largely abandoned formal Christianity in his youth, adopted Sun-Yat-senism as a substitute religion in middle age, and in later life proclaimed his devotion to the Confucian tradition of ancestor worship. Paul Linebarger's mainstream novels, written and published in the 1940s, display no commitment to an orthodox religious faith. (The protagonist of *Ria* undergoes a vague mystical experience in the novel's closing pages, but she decides it has nothing to do with God.)

According to Linebarger's wife Genevieve, 'When we were married [in 1950] he knew I was religious, but he told me very honestly he was agnostic.' She said that Paul 'became particularly interested in religion after my mother's death [in 1955]. He was crazy about my mother. I think her death affected him as much or more than mine would have ... She died so bravely ... I know that was what persuaded him' (interview, 26 September 1979). Linebarger and his wife then chose to join the Episcopal Church, as a compromise between her Catholicism and his Protestant background. (His brother Wentworth recalls that Linebarger received some Episcopalian religious training at the Cathedral School in Shanghai when he was 7–9 years old. 'Paul liked it; he liked the structure of Episcopalianism' (interview, 26 March 1983).)

As J. J. Pierce has noted, Linebarger's early drafts on the underpeople do not show 'any religious element *at all*'.[30] Even in the published version of the most famous underpeople story, 'The Ballad of Lost C'mell' (written in 1960–1 but perhaps plotted earlier), their leader (an eagle-person named the E'telekeli) was depicted principally as a brilliant political conspirator rather than as a religious figure.

But as Linebarger's own religious interests deepened and as he became more active in the church, the religious components of the underpeople's political movement also intensified, until the E'telekeli stood revealed (in *Norstrilia* (1975), p. 247) as the almost god-like leader of a 'Holy Insurgency'. This melding of political and religious leadership had its appeal for a man whose father regarded Sun Yat-sen as the greatest human being who ever lived, and who had himself when fifteen written, 'Sun Yat-sen is above the gods, for the gods are silly things that we tumble or raise with every change in the course of our imagination while Sun – Oh! *he* is [so] firm and real and great and lasting that it is beyond my power to tell you!'[31] The mature Paul Linebarger, though he worked in the presidential campaigns of Robert Taft, Dwight Eisenhower, and Richard Nixon, never found an American political figure in whom he could fully invest his faith. Instead he invented the E'telekeli.

The significance of religion in Linebarger's personal life as well as in his stories appears to have become much stronger after his repeated brushes with death in 1960. He referred to 1960 as a 'year of disasters for me personally';[32] the disasters were mainly life-threatening physical illnesses. The most bizarre underpeople story of all, 'A Planet Named Shayol' (1961), drew heavily upon his subjective experiences as a patient undergoing one operation after another, heavily drugged or anaesthetized in various ways. (The story's working title was 'People Never Live Forever', a phrase repeated often and optimistically by one of the suffering characters.) During the remaining six years of Linebarger's life, as he looked for signs of long-term physical recovery but instead encountered further signs of mortality, his stories became increasingly religious, though not increasingly orthodox. Ultimately the stories went even beyond the underpeople's politico-religious quest for full equality with humans, to the strange visions of personal sacrifice and quasi-salvation in his last finished works.[33]

Linebarger's basic vision of the underpeople, while less eccentric in its religious content than those final stories, is hardly something one would assign as devotional reading to the average Sunday-school class. The dominant figure in the underpeople stories is not their religious leader, the E'telekeli, but one of his disciples, the stunningly beautiful and professionally seductive cat-woman C'mell. In three major works ('Alpha Ralpha Boulevard', 'The Ballad of Lost C'mell,' *Norstrilia*), a series of male human protagonists feel dangerously attracted to C'mell. In each case she somehow reciprocates the protagonist's interest, though she emphasizes that as an underperson she is forbidden love or marriage with a true human. Linebarger's classic early story, 'The Game of Rat and Dragon', had already wrestled with the lures and limits of psychological intimacy between man and cat, without finding a satisfactory solution. The invention of C'mell carried that intimacy further in Linebarger's imagination, though even then, with a cat-woman fully human in form, his imagination observed certain limits. (Publicly, at least. An early draft of *Norstrilia* depicts C'mell's first meeting with the human male protagonist: 'She realized, looking into his innocent and singularly wise eyes, that she was seeing a man for the first time, and that a man was looking at her for the very first time as a woman ... By morning, they were not only lovers but friends.'[34])

Paul Linebarger had many women friends in his lifetime, and his relationships with them were often passionate. In several significant instances, the relationships were with women clearly regarded by others as 'not of his own kind' – different in race, ethnic background, nationality. One woman was a Jew; at least one was Chinese; a particularly important one was a White Russian émigrée in Peking, of questionable reputation and nearly twice as old as he. These relationships usually ended sadly if not tragically. Even when he did meet and marry a woman with similar interests and a 'respectable' background, the two of them could not fully bridge the emotional gulf he had long experienced between himself and others. Well before the marriage ended, he seems to have become emotionally closer to the family cats than to his wife. (Similarly, his short story 'Nancy' (1959) depicts a man trying to maintain his sanity during a long-distance spaceship flight after his co-pilot has died; he has only two hamsters for company. 'The hamsters were his one hope. He thrust his face close to their cage and talked to them. He attributed moods to them. He tried to live their lives with them, all as if they were people.' When that doesn't work he fantasizes the perfect woman as his shipmate.)

Paul Linebarger clearly recognized that he could never get from a cat all he wanted from a human woman. But cats did give him psychological rewards that for a long time he was unable to obtain on a steady basis from women. He imagined C'mell as the best of cat and of woman. The underpeople may in turn be seen at one level as an elaborate rationale for his continued fantasizing of the cat-woman C'mell. Only in his last years could Linebarger imagine relationships with real human women as satisfying as the psychological relationships he had experienced with his cats – especially with the cat of cats, Melanie, who gave part of her name to C'mell and whom his second wife Genevieve described as 'Paul's little love' (interview, 26 September 1979).

CONCLUSION

The story of the underpeople ranges through thousands of years in the Cordwainer Smith future history. It involves religious martyrdom, telepathic espionage, enigmatic mysticism, and hardball politics. It depicts arrogant human brutality towards underpeople who are valued far less than human slaves, and intense but unconsummated love affairs between people and underpeople that become legendary across the populated universe. Like any other memorable literary creation, the story is not reducible to a single meaning or to a single source in its creator's experience.

As those who knew him casually or well have often emphasized, Paul Linebarger was not a simple man. His widow told me, 'He was the only true genius I've ever met.' His brother said more modestly, 'Paul was pretty complex.' His older daughter quoted his frequent self-assessment, 'a near-genius', and added that he was 'extremely complex'.[35] A final aspect of the underpeople's appeal to Linebarger himself seems to have been the sheer complexity of their relationships with each other, with the hominids from far-flung planets, and with the trumen of Earth. Their search for full freedom and equality remained unresolved, even across the vast expanses of time and space within which Linebarger set their story. Some critics have suggested that if he had lived longer than his fifty-three years, Linebarger would have reached an ultimate political, philosophical, and/or religious resolution to their search. More likely, given his appreciation for the value of creative ambiguity and his hard-earned sense of life's lack of neat endings, he would have confronted the underpeople and their fellow inhabitants of the universe with new challenges, new complexities.

NOTES

Many individuals have assisted me in exploring the life and work of Paul Linebarger. Among those whose help was particularly useful in the preparation of this essay were: Genevieve Linebarger, W. Wentworth Linebarger, Rosana (Linebarger) Hart, Marcia Linebarger, J. J. Pierce, Patricia Woelk, John K. Fairbank, the staff of the Hoover Institution Archives (Stanford University), and the staff of the Kenneth Spencer Research Library (University of Kansas). I would also like to thank the National Endowment for the Humanities and the Faculty Research Committee of the University of California, Davis, for funds that enabled me to travel to the research collections containing Paul Linebarger's papers. Quotations from previously unpublished works of Paul Linebarger are used by permission of Rosana Hart and Marcia Linebarger.

1 'Humanity Overtaken', unpublished manuscript, 20 January 1940; Hoover Institution Archives.
2 See *Ria* (1947), p. 32, and *Carola* (1948), pp. 214–22, both published under the pseudonym of Felix C. Forrest.
3 See 'Scanners Live in Vain' (1950), and 'Mark Elf', first published in 1957, reprinted in Cordwainer Smith,

The Instrumentality of Mankind (1979), hereafter cited as *Instrumentality*. The anachronistic mixture of Beasts, 'Unauthorized Men,' 'modified animals,' and other creatures in 'Queen of the Afternoon' (first published in 1978, reprinted in *Instrumentality*) resulted from Genevieve Linebarger's heavy rewriting of a 1955 fragment by her late husband. For full references to first printing and reprinting of Cordwainer Smith stories, see Bibliography.

4 Unpublished draft of *Star-Craving Mad*, 'What Went Before', 15 May 1958, p. 2; Spencer Research Library.

5 On 1 Janary 1929, aged 15, Linebarger wrote in his diary, 'May Science progress and a great author appear! At present there is only H. G. Wells!' (Hoover Institution Archives).

6 In his introduction to J. J. Pierce (ed), *The Best of Cordwainer Smith* (1975).

7 H. G. Wells, *The Island of Dr Moreau*, (1895), ch. 14.

8 A bull-man in 'Alpha Ralpha Boulevard' has had to have his horns cut off to make him look more human; but the narrator notes that as an unusual instance.

9 Stapledon raised but did not fully deal with issues, such as sexual feelings between human and animal, that Linebarger later carried considerably further in the underpeople stories. Leslie Fiedler has suggested that Stapledon's *Sirius* may in turn have been inspired by *The Island of Dr Moreau* (in *Olaf Stapledon: A Man Divided* (Oxford, 1983), p. 186).

10 First published in the magazine *Weird Tales*, the

story was reprinted in Leigh Brackett (ed.), *The Best of Edmond Hamilton* (1977).

11 One exception is Johan Heje, who discusses the underpeople's development in terms of Linebarger's literary revisions of a philosophically inadequate and thus artistically frustrating first-draft conceptualization ('On the Genesis of *Norstrilia*', *Extrapolation*, 30 (1989), pp. 146–55).

12 Anthony Lewis and the *New York Times, Portrait of a Decade: The Second American Revolution* (New York, 1965).

13 'John Foyster Talks with Arthur Burns', in Andrew Porter (ed.), *Exploring Cordwainer Smith* (New York, 1975), p. 19.

14 John Foyster, 'Cordwainer Smith', in Porter, *Exploring Cordwainer Smith*, p. 10.

15 Terry Dowling, 'The Lever of Life: Winning and Losing in the Fiction of Cordwainer Smith', *Science Fiction: A Review of Speculative Literature*, 4, 1 (1982), p. 15.

16 Gary K. Wolfe, 'The Best of Cordwainer Smith', in F. N. Magill (ed.), *Survey of Science Fiction Literature* (New York, 1979), p. 188.

17 Quoted by J. J. Pierce in 'Mr Forest of Incandescent Bliss: The Man behind Cordwainer Smith', *Speculation*, 33 (1971), p. 15.

18 'Twenty SAIS Years, an Informal Memoir', *SAIS Review*, 8, 1 (1963), pp. 37–8.

19 'Education and Diplomacy: Thirteen Years', *SAIS Review*, 5, 3 (1961), p. 8.

20 A black man in Linebarger's unpublished mainstream novel 'Journey in Search of a Destination'

(1946 manuscript, Spencer Research Library), is described in terms applicable to an underperson: 'His face was sad; his eyes were like the eyes of a thoughtful dog' (p. 59); 'a humble man stood confusing his dreams of hopeless beauty with his aching hopes for the regeneration of his people' (p. 136). But the novel's viewpoint characters regard this man with pity rather than with empathy.

21 For a brief account of the senior Linebarger's life and his influence on his son, see Alan C. Elms, 'The Creation of Cordwainer Smith', *Science-Fiction Studies*, 11 (1984), pp. 265–7, 270–1. Paul M. W. Linebarger was a US Federal District Judge in the Philippines at the time of his political conversion, and retained the honorific title 'Judge' throughout his life.

22 Paul M. A. Linebarger, Djang Chu, and Ardath W. Burks, *Far Eastern Governments and Politics*, 2nd edn (Princeton, 1956), p. 47. Linebarger was mainly responsible for writing this section of the book.

23 'Introduction to and outlines of "The Philosophy of Chaos"', unpublished manuscript, 25 October 1931, pp. 1–2; Hoover Institution Archives.

24 Kenneth Keniston, *Young Radicals* (New York, 1968).

25 Pierce, 'Mr Forest of Incandescent Bliss', p. 6.

26 Paul M. W. Linebarger, unpublished memoirs, p. 343; Hoover Institution Archives.

27 Manuscript versions of 'Overseas China and Kuomintang Vitality', plus editorial correspondence, are located in the Hoover Institution Archives.

28 Pierce, introduction to *Best of*, p. xiv; Dowling, 'The Lever of Life', p. 10.
29 Arthur Burns, 'Paul Linebarger', in Porter, *Exploring Cordwainer Smith*, p. 9.
30 'The Treasure of the Secret Cordwainer', *Science Fiction Review*, 48 (Fall 1983), p. 11.
31 Diary, 14 January 1929; Hoover Institution Archives.
32 Letter to Professor Tao, 18 April 1962; Hoover Institution Archives.
33 'Three to a Given Star' and 'On the Sand Planet', both originally published in 1965, reprinted in *Quest of the Three Worlds* (1966); 'Under Old Earth', first published in 1966, reprinted in *Best of*.
34 *Star-Craving Mad*, ch. 5, p. 11; Spencer Research Library.
35 Interviews with Genevieve Linebarger, 26 September 1979; W. Wentworth Linebarger, 26 March 1983; Rosana Hart, 7 November 1979.

The Language and Languages of Science Fiction

WALTER E. MEYERS

Not often has fashionable twentieth-century literature shown much faith in language. The influential critics of our time favour ironic and detached authors over earnest and involved ones, prefer ambiguous language to clear, and cherish defeat rather than victory as a theme. 'Serious' authors and critics alike take for granted that such means and ends are the only possible artistic responses to the cruel history of the century. That this pessimism extends to the artistic use of human language is easily demonstrated, and I will not duplicate here what has already been done so many times. But I will begin by observing that the science fiction authors who have been most highly praised in mainstream criticism share the mainstream's despair about language and its uses.

Consider, for example, the literal annihilation of language in William Burroughs' *Nova Express* (1964), in which a cataclysmic climax leaves only 'word dust'. Or John Barth's *Giles Goat-boy* (1966), in which the characters express the meaninglessness of language both symbolically and literally. A central computer shreds the sacred scriptures of the story as it delivers them, allowing the messianic title character to eat his words both in fact and in effect. An echo of the Orwellian slogans of *1984* – 'War Is Peace', 'Freedom is Slavery', 'Ignorance Is Strength' – shows up in *Giles Goat-boy*'s 'passage is flunking', the expression in the work's academic metaphor of 'salvation is damnation'. The language of Barth's characters is impotent to improve their condition: the central figure preaches loving self-denial, and things get rapidly worse; he preaches self-indulgence, and things still get rapidly worse. Only when he ceases to preach – ceases, that is, to communicate – does normalcy return, in which things get worse, but slowly. Human communication hopelessly, inevitably fails.

Some themes of Doris Lessing are strikingly similar, most clearly in *Documents Relating to the Sentimental Agents in the Volyen Empire* (1983). In this fifth work of her 'Shikasta' series, the simple fact that language can be used to tell lies leads to the diagnosis that language is itself infected, that because rhetoric can be put to bad ends, rhetoric itself is *the* disease. Among the examples of pathological language the reader is invited to examine are Churchill's address to the British people during the Battle of Britain and the song of the American Civil Rights movement, 'We Shall Overcome'. Kurt Vonnegut expresses a similar view of human language in *Galapagos* (1985): a million years in the future, humanity has evolved into semi-intelligent seal-like creatures who loll on the beach, feed on raw fish in the sea, and live about thirty years. The book's narrator obsessively tells us that the problem with us ur-people was our big brains, which 'found it easy to . . . lie and lie' (p. 64).

Both the Argentinian Jorge Luis Borges and the Polish Stanislaw Lem have raised the review of non-existent books to an art form, Borges playfully but Lem, one suspects, more pessimistically. His *One Human Minute* (1986) consists of just such reviews, and at its very start we see 'Lem's Law': 'No one reads; if someone does read, he doesn't understand; if he understands, he immediately forgets.' Lem's romance *Solaris* (1961) is grounded in the impossibility of understanding an alien being – and one wonders if the book is not a metaphor for the impossibility of understanding other humans.

Perhaps the attitude of these writers to language – and some others could be added to the list – explains their critical popularity. Like their counterparts in mainstream literature, these science fiction writers doubt the possibility of useful, truthful communication; I do not think it is coincidental that Vonnegut, Lessing, Lem, Barth, and Burroughs are taken very seriously indeed by current criticism.

However, readers unfamiliar with science fiction may be surprised by a seemingly strange contradiction: these writers are much less highly regarded *within* science-fiction circles. Some aficionados of the form in fact deny that these writers write science fiction at all, and one of the striking differences between Vonnegut et al. And other science fiction writers is that the former distrust language while the latter revel in it.

We can look at language, therefore, to probe this difference between the two kinds of writers, and we can begin by observing that, on the whole, science fiction as a form is generally optimistic about language and frequently explores the uses, restrictions, potential – indeed, almost any facet – of language.

Science fiction can hardly help being concerned with language, since so many of its staple plots raise linguistic questions and have done so since the beginning. The monster of Mary Shelley's *Frankenstein* (1818) was in a real sense an 'alien' being: before it could communicate, it had to learn first human speech then human writing; time machines from H. G. Wells's on invite questions about the change of language through history; the exotic languages of dwellers on other worlds were imaginatively created in science fiction before the communication system of earthly bees was understood. Readers unfamiliar with the genre may think of it simply as cowboys-and-Indians-in-outer-space, and therefore may be surprised to find that science fiction most often asks questions first and shoots later.

Science fiction may deal with language in several

ways: the most peripheral of these is to use some linguistic practice or innovation simply as a detail that helps to establish an exotic setting. As Gene Wolfe says,

> Ever since *The Shadow of the Torturer* was published, people who like it have been asking, 'Which words are real, and which are made-up?' And people who don't, ask, 'Why did you use so many funny words?' The answers are that all the words are real, and I used odd words to convey the flavor of an odd place at an odd time. (*The Castle of the Otter* (1982), p. 25)

Some of them are odd indeed: the reader of chapter 1 will encounter *barbican, gallipots, simple* (as a noun), *mystes, badelaire, dhole, amschaspand*, and *arctother*. Yet Wolfe only mines the staggering richness of English vocabulary: 'In writing science fiction about unknown planets, the author is usually compelled to invent wonders and to name them. It occurred to me when I began *The Book of the New Sun* that Urth [his fictional world] has already wonders enough – if only it has inherited the wonders of Earth' (p. 40). All of his strange terms can be found in an unabridged dictionary.

Wolfe's use of unusual words is not, however, particularly characteristic of science fiction. A potboiler like James Clavell's *Shogun*, set in the sixteenth century, uses Japanese for exactly the same purpose. But the use of language in science fiction can go beyond adding colour to the setting.

A linguistic detail used in an off-handed way may imply a technology far beyond that now available, thereby strikingly demonstrating that the time of the story is not our time and reminding us that its characters' ways may not be our ways. In George Alec Effinger's *When Gravity Fails* (1987), a character explains *daddies*, very small machines that plug directly into the skull: '"Daddy is what we call an add-on. A daddy gives you temporary knowledge. Say you chip in a Swedish-language daddy; then you understand Swedish until you pop it out. Shopkeepers, lawyers, and other con men all use daddies,"' (p. 2). The time may be a century in advance of our own time; the characters' clothing, speech, habits, motivations, and so on, are like our own. If the surface similarity of culture allows the reader to be lulled into a feeling of familiarity, the inclusion of a detail like the *daddy* shatters that familiarity, unsettling him and reawakening an alert awareness. In William Gibson's *Count Zero* (1986), the time is again the near future. An American character is traveling in Mexico; it would be the easiest thing in the world to make the character fluent in Spanish – at least enough to get along. But Gibson uses the plug-in: 'Among the dozen-odd microsofts the Dutchman had given him was one that would allow a limited fluency in Spanish, but in Vallarta he'd fumbled behind his left ear and inserted a dustplug instead, hiding the socket and plug beneath a square of flesh-tone micropore' (p. 3). Why not make the character fluent in Spanish in the usual way? Because if Gibson did that, he would have neglected an opportunity to remind the reader that the story, being science fiction, is open-ended – potentially full of imaginative surprises that naturalistic fiction cannot give.

Even if we accept some of the premises of naturalistic fiction, we can easily justify some of the practices of science fiction. Hugo Gernsback, a native of Luxemburg who emigrated to the United States, in 1926 published *Amazing Stories*, the first pulp-magazine devoted to science fiction. Although the stories he printed may have left much to be desired, Gernsback was a fervent if innocent believer in the power of the genre to promote scientific careers among the young. His goal may have been naive and may often have produced wretched fiction, but his means – an insistence on the inclusion of science in the stories – can be justified on literary grounds far more pragmatic: science is a part of our lives, like it or not, and a fiction that imitates life must include science. And this observation leads us to a second use of language in science fiction, a use far more sophisticated: when some aspect of language is itself the subject of the story.

Paul J. McAuley's *Four Hundred Billion Stars* (1988) is such a story. Set centuries in the future on a world orbiting a red giant star, it tells a story that begins like a recounting of Champollion's discovery of the Rosetta Stone. Alien structures have been found on the planet, built perhaps hundreds of thousands of years ago; the plot demands an urgent deciphering of the inscriptions lining the structure. As these are artefacts of an alien civilization probably far more different from us than the Incas were from Pizarro, we can expect the task to be difficult, perhaps in unforeseen ways. As the exploration team's linguist says, 'The written language, at least, is very complicated. There are at least sixty-four graphemes, and I have catalogued more than a thousand ideograms as well. You are Japanese, so I do not have to tell you how difficult such a written language can be. Depending upon the context, a single ideogram may represent half a dozen disparate notions' (p. 158). And later, 'It turns out that the script is set out as a kind of musical notation; that's why Ramaro was having so much trouble with it' (p. 177). Still later, 'It was a single line, a flowing unbroken script like an incredibly complicated trace from an electroencephalogram, characters and ideograms flowing one into the other, clustered in groups of four, each group a single concept, each concept part of a greater group just as DNA codes for amino acids that, linked together, make a protein that in turn twists and coils, primary, secondary, tertiary spirals which determine its final functional form' (p. 184).

As it happens, the linguistic method of McAuley's

team is highly questionable, but its deficiencies would hardly be noticeable to the average intelligent reader. One could not use the text (as Gernsback might have wished) for elementary instruction in how to decipher a dead language, but McAuley's terminology is the terminology of linguistics: terms like *grapheme* and *ideogram* illustrate what H. G. Wells called 'the ingenious use of scientific patter'. The story does not have to *be* scientific, it only has to *sound* scientific in order to work: in this case to demonstrate that the organized body of knowledge that we call science is the characters' chief tool and that communication is their chief desire.

When the author is knowledgeable about the subject, the linguistics of science fiction can be very sound indeed. I mentioned above that because science is part of our world, even the most realistic of fictions would seem obliged to take it into account. Merely in order to mirror reality, fiction needs to encompass such real-world events as the fact, for example, that I am essentially communicating with a computer in the very mundane task of writing this essay. If the notion of communicating with aliens seems far-fetched, consider the computer as a kind of alien, as Paul Preuss does in *Human Error* (1985).

His hero, Toby Bridgeman, is a present-day British computer programmer working (as many currently are) on the development of Artificial Intelligence. His program, if successful, will advance this infant endeavour by giving the machine an essentially human linguistic capacity – the ability to recognize a pun. Toby supplies the machine with a riddle: 'The big moron and the little moron were walking along the edge of a cliff. The big moron fell off. Why didn't the little moron?' The machine at first answers correctly, 'Because he was a little more on.' The second time Toby tries, the machine answers 'Because she was a little more on.' Toby thinks, 'what's this "she"? Is the machine exhibiting nonsexist tendencies, or is it waffling?' (p. 13).

If the immediate goal – to recognize a pun – seems trivial, Toby's final goal is much more ambitious, and Preuss explains why: Toby is attempting 'to shape programs that could generate diverse descriptions of linguistic objects and relate them in ways not only logical but, as Toby dearly hoped, pragmatic – and maybe creative as well.' As the character argues,

> The higher – the more 'perfect'–the organism, the more slowly it developed . . . and the same was true of programs capable of learning from experience. Only by acquiring knowledge about the world and expressing that knowledge in words, by experiencing success and failure in using words to influence the course of events – by talking up a storm and taking the consequences, like any two-year-old – only thus could a machine master language, beyond a few stock phrases manipulated according to structural rules of

> limited flexibility. Only by combining experience of language and the real world had a machine, on two occasions now – and here Toby dared hint at what was uppermost on his mind – been able to understand a pun. (p. 16)

But when asked the riddle for the third time, the machine answers, 'Because it was not near the edge.' '"Balls," said Toby' (p. 17).

In *Human Error*, Preuss shows a knowledge of both natural and artificial languages and about human acquisition of language – self-acquisition – as a possible model for the development of computers that could not merely respond but truly communicate.

Such a machine occurs in a story that illustrates the highest use of linguistics in science fiction, a use that happens when language establishes the setting and serves as subject matter, and to these two functions adds a third: reflection on human communication itself. Until the intelligent computer or alien shows up, language is a particularly human activity: the more we understand it, the better we understand ourselves. This third kind of story helps us to understand both the linguistic mask we present to the world and the human face that lies behind it.

This essay is purposely limited to what is popularly called science fiction, but modern fantasy shares many of the same preoccupations with language. J. R. R. Tolkien's monumental cycle of stories of Middle-earth, for example, devotes far more attention to beings he calls Elves than it does to Hobbits. The name of those creatures in their own language is *Quendi*, a word which translates into English as 'speakers'. They are the original namers in Middle-earth, the race that gives the gift of language to others, and their own name – like others in the cycle – expresses the core of their nature: they understand and enter into communion with everything in nature around them – they speak. It is this sense of *speak*, I think, that enspirits the title of Orson Scott Card's work, *Speaker for the Dead* (1986), my example for the third function of language in science fiction.

Speaker for the Dead is linguistically sophisticated in a variety of directions: something like three thousand years in the future, human society has brought its many languages to a hundred worlds. For example, a development of English called Stark is the second or school language of humanity; Nordic, a descendant of Swedish, figures peripherally; and Portuguese is the language of the colony where the main action occurs. Just as Card's linguistic universe is current and plausible, so is his physical universe: it is Einsteinian – nothing travels faster than the speed of light although ships may very closely approach it. Because one's subjective time slows down the faster one moves, travel from one planet to another may seem a matter of weeks to its passengers but years elapse on the planets of departure and arrival. The interstellar isolation of language communities positively invites the development first of dialects and eventually of mutually unintelligible languages. But languages in the story have not changed as much as we might have expected. Card borrows a convention from Ursula Le Guin – a machine called the ansible. As his narrator observes, 'If it weren't for the ansible, providing instantaneous communication among the Hundred Worlds, we could not possibly maintain a common language. Interstellar travel is far too rare and slow. Stark would splinter into ten thousand dialects within a century. It might be interesting to have the computers run a projection of linguistic changes on Lusitania, if Stark were allowed to decay and absorb Portuguese' (pp. 4–5).

The concentration on human languages at the beginning is an ironic contrast to the fact that in all its explorations, humanity has discovered only two speaking alien races. The first of these, the 'buggers', bears this nickname reminiscent of the menacing monsters of pulp-magazine covers. Their appearance, their name, their very other-ness prevented communication, leading to misunderstanding, leading to war, leading to the extermination of the race at human hands. The particular hands were those of Andrew Wiggin, prophetically nicknamed 'Ender'. *Speaker for the Dead* is a sequel to *Ender's Game* (1985), which details how Ender as a child unwittingly but directly brought about the genocide of the buggers. The second book is the story of his expiation for that deed.

In the second story, a quasi-religious practice has grown up: a Speaker for the Dead is a kind of priest or sage who on request attends a funeral and, through speaking the truth about the deceased as completely and truthfully as possible, tries to reconcile the memory of the dead to the community. Speakers for the Dead bring little but understanding, and sometimes that understanding brings grief, in which case the Speaker has the additional duty of trying to heal the pains he has caused. Although three thousand years have passed since the killing of the buggers, Andrew Wiggin is only in his thirties, time having slowed for him during his many journeys. 'Ender' has become a hated, almost legendary figure, and only a handful of people know that Andrew Wiggin is Ender, not *a* speaker for this dead man or that dead woman, but *the* speaker for the race killed by humanity.

Andrew Wiggin is accompanied by a matured artificial consciousness: through a small communicating device, he is always in contact with 'Jane', a disembodied intelligence who resides – if that is the right word – in the manifold layers of the ansible communication network. Although she has been self-aware for many centuries, she has not revealed her existence until recently. The reason for her self-effacement is simple:

> The computers of the Hundred Worlds were hands and feet, eyes and ears to her. She spoke every language that had ever been committed to computers, and read every book in every library on every world. She learned that human beings had long been afraid that someone like her would come to exist: in all the stories she was hated, and her coming meant either her certain murder or the destruction of mankind. Even before she was born, human beings had imagined her, and, imagining her, slain her a thousand times.

'So she give them no sign that she was alive' (pp. 66–7). Besides Jane, Wiggin carries on his travels the cocoon of a fertilized queen of the buggers. In atonement for his extermination of the race, he searches for the right planet on which to release the cocoon and allow the species to live again. Through him, Card subtly makes the point that communication is as much listening as speaking: the other humans speak to him by voice, Jane by radio, and the hive-queen telepathically. Slow to condemn, ready to listen, he is a junction, a crossroads for the exploration of language in the book, and he is also ready to prevent a second genocide when, in *Speaker for the Dead*, humans encounter a second intelligent, language-using race.

At the start, things do not seem hopeful: this species is again de-humanized – trivialized – by a nickname based on their appearance: the piggies. But the trauma of the killing of the buggers has been long-lasting: contact with the piggies is timid, restricted by a host of regulations intended to keep them primitive and thereby harmless. But neither their intellect nor their linguistic capability is primitive: 'We have identified four piggy languages,' writes one linguist in a professional journal.

> The 'Males' Language' is the one we have most commonly heard. We have also heard snatches of 'Wives' Language', which they apparently use to converse with the females (how's that for sexual differentiation!), and 'Tree Language', a ritual idiom that they say is used in praying to the ancestral totem trees. They have also mentioned a fourth language, called 'Father Tongue', which apparently consists of beating different-sized sticks together. They insist that it is a real language, as different from the others as Portuguese is from English. They may call it Father Tongue because it's done with sticks of wood, which come from trees, and they believe that trees contain the spirits of their ancestors. (p. 61)

The names the linguist has given to the language show a human bias: the very term 'Males' Language' suggests the similar, sexually-based manner of speech used by some primitive tribes on earth. But the piggies' method of reproduction is wholly unsuspected by the human characters at this point, and the adoption of the human term will be a stumbling-block in the humans' understanding of the characters.

The story is not resolved until the two races are able to understand each other, and that understanding is not achieved until they have a common language: language is the pathway to communion.

Speaker for the Dead, like *Human Error* or *Four Hundred Billion Stars*, has an ending whose maturity and profundity we tend to dismiss by labelling it 'happy'. But it is the kind of ending that describes success, even if limited and bought at great price, rather than failure. It is an ending optimistic rather than pessimistic, an ending that stresses the beauty of our best desires rather than our distance from them. And such an ending, call it what you will, is frequent in science fiction, a frequency demonstrated by the intentional limitation of examples to stories of only the past few years. Many more could be added to those briefly discussed here: just three of those many would include Greg Bear's *Blood Music* (1985), which explores communication not just with intelligent computers but with an intelligent virus; Russell Hoban's brilliant *Riddley Walker* (1980), written entirely in a 'future' dialect of English; and the Ozark trilogy (*Twelve Fair Kingdoms, The Grand Jubilee*, and *And Then There'll Be Fireworks*, all 1981) by Suzette Haden Elgin, herself an academic linguist, in which language is both subject and means for an exploration of sexual relations. And it should be kept in mind that no matter how seemingly wild the situation in these stories, their speculation (from *speculum*, 'mirror') reflects us – it is our language that we hear echoing from these creatures of our imagination.

If we are creatures whose choices are limited to killing or talking then this genre – science fiction, which places such confidence in our ability to speak truthfully and to good effect, which places such confidence in the capacity of language to serve well – then this genre has already voted for the latter choice.

Bibliography

WORKS OF FICTION CITED

Note: science fiction, as a field, is full of bibliographical traps or impossibilities. Many stories were originally published in ephemeral magazines which never reached even copyright libraries; reprinting is very common, but authors often seize the chance of making major alterations to suit a new format; retitling is also common; and many novels have appeared prior to book publication as serials in magazines, or as separate stories. In these circumstances I have tried to give details of first publication for books, and for stories where this is ascertainable; but also to indicate convenient collections or accessible reprints where first editions are unavailable and guidance seems needed, and where contributors have given page references to particular editions; and to give information about pseudonyms and alternative titles where this is likely to be useful.

Ballard, J. G., *The Drowned World*, Berkley, New York, 1962; reprinted Penguin, Harmondsworth, 1965.

Ballard, J. G., 'The Terminal Beach', in Ballard's col-

lection *The Terminal Beach*, Gollancz, London, 1964.
Barth, John, *Giles Goat-boy*, Doubleday, Garden City, NY, 1966.
Bear, Greg, *Blood Music*, Arbor House, New York, 1985.
Bishop, Michael, *Philip K. Dick Is Dead, Alas*, Grafton, London, 1988.
Brin, David, *The Postman*, Bantam, New York, 1985.
Budrys, Algis, *Some Will Not Die*, Regency Books, Evanston, Ill., 1961.
Burkett, William, *Sleeping Planet*, Doubleday, Garden City, NY, 1965; originally serialized in *Analog*, July–September 1964.
Burroughs, William, *Nova Express*, Grove Press, New York, 1964.
Capek, Karel, *War with the Newts*, first published (in Czech) 1936, trans. by M. and R. Weatherall, Allen and Unwin, London, 1937.
Card, Orson Scott, *Ender's Game*, TOR, New York, 1985.
Card, Orson Scott, *Speaker for the Dead*, TOR, New York, 1986.
Clarke, Arthur C., *Childhood's End*, Ballantine, New York, 1953; reprinted Ballantine, New York, 1974.
Crowley, John, *Engine Summer*, Doubleday, Garden City, NY, 1979; reprinted Methuen, London, 1982.
Davidson, Avram, 'Bumberboom', *Fantasy and Science Fiction*, December 1966.
Dick, Philip K., *Do Androids Dream of Electric Sheep?*, Doubleday, Garden City, NY, 1968.
Disch, Thomas, *Camp Concentration*, Hart-Davis, London, 1968.

Effinger, George Alec, *When Gravity Fails*, Arbor House, New York, 1987.

Elgin, Suzette Haden, *Twelve Fair Kingdoms*, Doubleday, New York, 1981.

Elgin, Suzette Haden, *The Grand Jubilee*, Doubleday, New York, 1981.

Elgin, Suzette Haden, *And Then There'll Be Fireworks*, Doubleday, New York, 1981.

Engh, M. T., *A Wind from Bukhara*, Grafton Books, London, 1989; originally published as *Arslan*, Warner, New York, 1976.

Forrest, Felix C. [pseudonym of Paul M. A. Linebarger], *Ria*, Duell, Sloan and Pearce, New York, 1947.

Forrest, Felix C., *Carola*, Duell, Sloan and Pearce, New York, 1948.

Gibson, William, *Neuromancer*, Ace Books, New York, 1984.

Gibson, William, *Count Zero*, Arbor House, New York, 1986.

Haldeman, Joe, *War Year*, Holt, Rinehart and Wilson, New York, 1972; revised paperback reprint Pocket Books, New York, 1978.

Haldeman, Joe, *The Forever War*, Ballantine, New York, 1974, reprinted Orbit, London, 1976. The first two sections appeared in *Analog* as 'Hero' (June 1972) and 'We Are Very Happy Here' (November 1973).

Haldeman, Joe (ed.), *Study War No More*, St Martin's Press, New York, 1977.

Haldeman, Joe (ed.), *Body Armor 2000*, Ace Books, New York, 1986.

Hamilton, Edmond, 'Day of Judgement', first published in *Weird Tales*, September 1946, later reprinted in

Fiction

Leigh Brackett (ed.), *The Best of Edmond Hamilton*, Nelson Doubleday, New York, 1977.

Harrison, Harry, *Bill the Galactic Hero*, Gollancz, London, 1965.

Harrison, Harry, *Bill the Galactic Hero on the Planet of Robot Slaves*, Avon, New York, 1989.

Heinlein, Robert A., 'Let There Be Light', first published in *Super Science Stories*, May 1940, later reprinted in Heinlein's collection *The Man Who Sold the Moon*, Shasta, Chicago, 1950.

Heinlein, Robert A., *The Day After Tomorrow*, New American Library, New York, 1958; first published in book form as *Sixth Column*, Gnome Press, New York, 1949, but with prior serialization in *Astounding Science Fiction*, 1941.

Heinlein, Robert A., *Starman Jones*, G. P. Putnam's, New York, 1953.

Heinlein, Robert A., *Starship Troopers*, G. P. Putnam's, New York, 1959; reprinted New American Library, New York, 1967.

Hoban, Russell, *Riddley Walker*, Summit, New York, 1980; reprinted Washington Square, New York, 1982.

Kornbluth, Cyril M., *Christmas Eve*, Michael Joseph, London, 1956; originally published as *Not This August*, Doubleday, Garden City, NY, 1955.

Kornbluth, Cyril M., see also Pohl, Frederik.

Le Guin, Ursula K., *The Left Hand of Darkness*, Walker, New York, 1969.

Le Guin, Ursula K., 'The Word for World is Forest', first published in Harlan Ellison (ed.), *Again, Dangerous Visions*, Doubleday, Garden City, NY, 1972; also printed separately by Berkley, New York, 1972.

Le Guin, Ursula K., *The Dispossessed*, Harper and Row, New York, 1974.

Le Guin, Ursula K., 'The New Atlantis', in Robert Silverberg (ed.), *The New Atlantis and other Novellas of Science Fiction*, Hawthorn Books, New York, 1975; reprinted in Le Guin's collection *The Compass Rose*, Harper and Row, New York, 1982.

Lem, Stanislaw, *Solaris*, first published (in Polish), 1961, trans. by Joanna Kilmartin and Steve Cox, Faber and Faber, London, 1970.

Lem, Stanislaw, *One Human Minute*, Harcourt Brace Jovanovich, San Diego, Calif., 1986.

Lessing, Doris, *Documents Relating to the Sentimental Agents in the Volyen Empire*, Alfred A. Knopf, New York, 1983.

Linebarger, Paul M. A., See Smith, Cordwainer and Forrest, Felix C.

McAuley, Paul J., *Four Hundred Billion Stars*, Gollancz, London, 1988.

McQuay, Mike, *Jitterbug*, Bantam, New York, 1984.

Niven, Larry, *A World Out of Time*, Holt, Rinehart and Winston, New York, 1976.

Niven, Larry and Pournelle, Jerry, *Footfall*, Ballantine, New York, 1985.

Orwell, George, *Coming Up for Air*, Gollancz, London, 1939; reprinted Penguin, Harmondsworth, 1962.

Pohl, Frederik, *The Years of the City*, Timescape, New York,1984

Pohl, Frederik, 'Criticality', *Analog*, December 1984.

Pohl, Frederik, *Black Star Rising*, Ballantine, New York, 1985.

Pohl, Frederik, *The Coming of the Quantum Cats*,

Bantam, New York, 1986; originally serialized in *Analog*, January–April 1986.

Pohl, Frederik, and Kornbluth, Cyril M., *The Space Merchants*, Ballantine, New York, 1953; originally published in shortened form as a two-part serial in *Galaxy*, 1952, as *Gravy Planet*.

Preuss, Paul, *Human Error*, TOR, New York, 1985.

Pynchon, Thomas, *The Crying of Lot 49*, Lippincott, Philadelphia, 1966.

Robinson, Kim, *The Wild Shore*, Ace Books, New York, 1984.

Robinson, Kim S., *The Gold Coast*, TOR, New York, 1988.

Shelley, Mary W., *Frankenstein, or the Modern Prometheus*, Lackington, Hughes et al., London, 1818.

Shelley, Mary W., *The Last Man*, Henry Colburn, London, 1826; reprinted with an introduction by Brian Aldiss, Hogarth Press, London, 1985.

Smith, Cordwainer [pseudonym of Paul M.A. Linebarger], *Space Lords*, Pyramid, New York, 1965.

Smith, Cordwainer, *Quest of the Three Worlds*, Ace Books, New York, 1966. Includes stories originally published as 'Three to a Given Star' (*Galaxy*, October 1965) and 'On the Sand Planet' (*Amazing*, December 1965).

Smith, Cordwainer, *Norstrilia*, Ballantine, New York, 1975.

Smith, Cordwainer, *The Best of Cordwainer Smith*, ed. J. J. Pierce, Nelson Doubleday, Garden City, NY, 1975. Contains among other stories 'Scanners Live in Vain' (*Fantasy Book*, June 1950), 'The Game of Rat and Dragon' (*Galaxy*, October 1955), 'Alpha Ralpha

Boulevard,' (*Fantasy and Science Fiction*, June 1961), 'A Planet Named Shayol' (*Galaxy*, October 1961). 'The Ballad of Lost C'mell' (*Galaxy*, October 1962), 'The Dead Lady of Clown Town' (*Galaxy*, August 1964), 'Under Old Earth' (*Galaxy*, February 1966).

Smith, Cordwainer, *The Instrumentality of Mankind*, Ballantine, New York, 1979. Contains among other stories 'Mark Elf' (*Saturn*, May 1957), 'Nancy' (*Satellite SF*, March 1959), 'Queen of the Afternoon' (*Galaxy*, April 1978).

Spinrad, Norman, 'The Lost Continent', first published in Anthony Cheetham (ed.), *Science against Man*, Avon Books, New York, 1970, later reprinted in Spinrad's collections *No Direction Home*, Pocket Books, New York, 1975, and *The Star-Spangled Future*, Ace Books, New York, 1979.

Spinrad, Norman, 'A Thing of Beauty', first published in *Analog*, January 1973, later reprinted in the 1975 and 1979 Spinrad collections cited above.

Stapledon, W. Olaf, *Last and First Men: A Story of the Near and Far Future*, Methuen, London, 1930; reprinted Dover, New York, 1968.

Stapledon, W. Olaf, *Sirius: A Fantasy of Love and Discord*, Secker and Warburg, London, 1944.

Stewart, George R., *Earth Abides*, Random House, New York, 1949; reprinted Fawcett, New York, 1971.

Tevis, Walter, *Mockingbird*, Doubleday, New York, 1980.

Tucker, Wilson, *The Long Loud Silence*, Rinehart, New York, 1952.

Turner, George, *The Sea and Summer*, Faber and Faber, London, 1987, reprinted as *Drowning Towers*, Arbor House, New York, 1988.

Vinge, Vernor, *The Peace War*, Bluejay Books, New York, 1984.

Vonnegut, Kurt, *Galapagos*, Jonathan Cape, London, 1985.

Wells, H.G., *The Time Machine: An Invention*, Heinemann, London, 1895.

Wells, H.G., *The Island of Dr Moreau*, Heinemann, London, 1896.

Wolfe, Gene, *The Shadow of the Torturer*, Timescape, New York, 1980.

Wolfe, Gene, *The Claw of the Conciliator*, Timescape, New York, 1981.

Wolfe, Gene, *The Sword of the Lictor*, Timescape, New York, 1981.

Wolfe, Gene, *The Citadel of the Autarch*, Timescape, New York, 1982.

Wolfe, Gene, *The Castle of the Otter*, Ziesing Brothers, Willimantic, Connecticut, 1982.

Zamyatin, Yevgeny, *We*, written (in Russian) 1920, trans. by Gregory Zilboorg for Dutton, New York, 1924, and (among others) by Mirra Ginsburg for Viking, New York, 1972.

HISTORICAL AND CRITICAL WORKS CITED

Aldiss, Brian W., with Wingrove, David, *Trillion Year Spree: The History of Science Fiction*, Atheneum, New York, 1986.

Ash, Brian (ed.), *The Visual Encyclopaedia of Science Fiction*, Pan, London, 1977.

Barthes, Roland, *Mythologies*, Editions du Seuil, Paris, 1957, selected and translated by Annette Lavers, Paladin, London, 1973.

Baudrillard, Jean, *The Mirror of Production*, Telos Press, St Louis, 1974.

Baudrillard, Jean, *For a Critique of the Political Economy of the Sign*, Telos Press, St Louis, 1981.

Bedini, Silvio A., 'The Evolution of Science Museums', *Technology and Culture*, 6 (Winter 1965), pp. 1–29.

Bell, Daniel (ed.), *The Radical Right*, Arno Press, New York, 2nd edn. 1962.

Bondella, Peter and Musa, Mark (eds), *The Portable Machiavelli*, Penguin, London, 1979.

Bourdieu, Pierre, *Distinction: A Social Critique of the Judgement of Taste*, trans. by Richard Nice, Harvard UP, Cambridge, Mass., 1984.

Brooks, Peter, 'Freud's Masterplot', in Robert Con Davis and Ronald Schleifer (eds), *Contemporary Literary Criticism: Literary and Cultural Studies*, Longman, New York and London, 1989.

Brosnan, John, *Future Tense*, St Martin's, New York, 1978.

Carter, Dale, *The Final Frontier: The Rise and Fall of the American Rocket State*, Verso, London, 1988.

Crossley, Robert, *H. G. Wells*, Starmont, Mercer Island, Wash., 1986.

Delany, Samuel R., *An American Shore*, Dragon Press, Elizabethtown, NY, 1978.

De Man, Paul, *The Rhetoric of Romanticism*, Columbia UP, New York, 1984.

Dowling, Terry, 'The Lever of Life: Winning and Losing in the Fiction of Cordwainer Smith', *Science Fiction: A Review of Speculative Literature*, 4, 1 (1982), pp. 9–37.

Ellis, John, *The Sharp End of War*, Corgi, London, 1982.

History and Critcism

Elms, Alan C., 'The Creation of Cordwainer Smith', *Science-Fiction Studies*, 11 (1984), pp. 264–83.

Fiedler, Leslie, *Olaf Stapledon: A Man Divided*, Oxford UP, Oxford, 1983.

Foster, Hal (ed.), *The Anti-Aesthetic: Essays on Post-modern Culture*, Bay Press, Port Townsend, Wash., 1983.

Franklin, H. Bruce, *Robert A. Heinlein: America as Science Fiction*, Oxford UP, New York, 1980.

Geduld, Harry M. (ed.), *The Definitive Time Machine: A Critical Edition of H. G. Wells's Scientific Romance*, Indiana UP, Bloomington, Ind., 1987.

Gordon, Joan, *Joe Haldeman: Starmont Reader's Guide*, Starmont Press, Seattle, 1980.

Haldeman, Joe, 'Science Fiction and War', *Isaac Asimov's Science Fiction Magazine*, April 1986.

Hassan, Ihab, *The Dismemberment of Orpheus: Towards a Postmodern Literature*, Oxford UP, London, 1971.

Heje, Johan, 'On the Genesis of *Norstrilia*', *Extrapolation*, 30 (1989), pp. 146–55.

Hudson, Kenneth, *Museums of Influence*, Cambridge UP, Cambridge, 1987.

Huntington, John, *The Logic of Fantasy: H. G. Wells and Science Fiction*, Columbia UP, New York, 1982.

Impey, Oliver and MacGregor, Arthur (eds), *The Origins of Museums: The Cabinet of Curiosities in Sixteenth-and Seventeenth-Century Europe*, Clarendon, Oxford, 1985.

Keniston, Kenneth, *Young Radicals: Notes on Committed Youth*, Harcourt, Brace and World, New York, 1968.

Kinkead, Eugene, *In Every War But One*, W. W. Norton, New York, 1959.

Kissinger, Henry, *Nuclear Weapons and Foreign Policy*, Harper, New York, 1957.

Kroeber, Karl, *Romantic Fantasy and Science Fiction*, Yale UP, New Haven, 1988.

Lefanu, Sarah, *In the Chinks of the World Machine: Feminism and Science Fiction*, The Women's Press, London, 1988.

Lewis, Anthony, and the *New York Times*, *Portrait of a Decade: The Second American Revolution*, Random House, New York, 1964.

Linebarger, Paul M. A., 'Education and Diplomacy: Thirteen Years', *School of Advanced International Studies Review*, 5, 3 (1961), pp. 4–11.

Linebarger, Paul M. A., 'Twenty SAIS Years, an Informal Memoir', *SAIS Review*, 8, 1 (1963), pp. 4–40.

Linebarger, Paul M. A., Chu, Djang and Burks, Ardath W., *Far Eastern Governments and Politics*, Van Nostrand, Princeton, 2nd edn 1956.

Lundwall, Sam, *Science Fiction: What's It All About?*, Ace Books, New York, 1971.

Lyotard, Jean-Francois, *The Postmodern Condition: A Report on Knowledge*, Manchester UP, Manchester, 1979.

Miller, Edward, *That Noble Cabinet: A History of the British Museum*, Andre Deutsch, London, 1973.

Moskin, J. Robert, *The Story of the US Marine Corps*, Paddington Press, New York, 1979.

Myers, Thomas, *Walking Point*, Oxford UP, Oxford, 1989.

Nelson, Cary and Grossberg, Lawrence (eds), *Marxism and the Interpretation of Culture*, Macmillan, London, 1988.

Osgood, Robert E., *Limited War: The Challenge to American Strategy*, University of Chicago Press, Chicago, 1957.

Page, Norman, *Speech in the English Novel*, Longman, London, 1973.

Panshin, Alexei, *Heinlein in Dimension*, Advent, Chicago, 1968.

Parrinder, Patrick, *Science Fiction: Its Criticism and Teaching*, Methuen, London, 1971.

Pierce, J. J., 'Mr. Forest of Incandescent Bliss: The Man behind Cordwainer Smith', *Speculation*, 33 (1971), pp. 2–23.

Pierce, J. J., 'The Treasure of the Secret Cordwainer', *Science Fiction Review*, 48 (Fall 1983), pp. 8–14.

Pohl, Frederik, *The Way the Future Was: A Memoir*, Ballantine, New York, 1978.

Porter, Andrew (ed.), *Exploring Cordwainer Smith*, Algol Press, New York, 1975.

Porush, David, *The Soft Machine: Cybernetic Fiction*, Methuen, New York, 1985.

Rose, Mark, *Alien Encounters: Anatomy of Science Fiction*, Harvard UP, Cambridge, Mass., 1981.

Schelling, Thomas, *Arms and Influence*, Yale UP, New Haven, 1966.

Scholes, Robert and Rabkin, Eric, *Science Fiction: History, Science, Fiction*, Oxford UP, London, 1977.

Shippey, T. A., 'The Cold War in Science Fiction, 1940–60', in Patrick Parrinder (ed.), *Science Fiction: A Critical Guide*, Longman, London, 1979, pp. 90–109.

Shippey, T. A., 'Semiotic Ghosts and Ghostlinesses in the Work of Bruce Sterling', in George Slusser (ed.), *Fiction 2000: Cyberpunk and the Future of Narrative*,

University of Michigan Research Press, Ann Arbor, forthcoming.

Society of Antiquaries of London, *Archaeologia*, 1 (1770).

Suerbaum, Ulrich, Broich, Ulrich and Borgmeier, Raimund, *Science Fiction*, Reclam, Stuttgart, 1981.

Suvin, Darko, *Metamorphoses of Science Fiction: On the Poetics and History of a Literary Genre*, Yale UP, New Haven, 1979.

Suvin, Darko, *Positions and Presuppositions in Science Fiction*, Macmillan, London, 1988.

Usborne, Richard, *Clubland Heroes*, Hutchinson, London, 1978.

Welch, Martin, 'The Ashmolean as Described by its Earliest Visitors', in Arthur MacGregor (ed.), *Tradescant's Rarities: Essays on the Foundation of the Ashmolean Museum*, Clarendon, Oxford, pp. 59–69.

Wells, H. G., *An Experiment in Autobiography*, 2 vols, Gollancz and Cresset Press, London, 1934.

Westin, Alan F., 'The John Birch Society' in Daniel Bell (ed.), *The Radical Right*, Arno Press, New York, 2nd edn 1962, pp. 201–27.

Williams, Raymond, *The Country and the City*, Chatto and Windus, London, 1973.

Wittlin, Alma S., *The Museum: Its History and Its Tasks in Education*, Routledge and Kegan Paul, London, 1949.

Wolfe, Gary K., 'The Best of Cordwainer Smith', in F. N. Magill (ed.), *Survey of Science Fiction Literature*, Salem Press, Englewood Cliffs, NJ, 1979, pp. 186–90.

Notes on Contributors

John Christie is Chairman of the History and Philosophy of Science Division at the University of Leeds. He has recently acted as editor of *The Figural and the Literal: Problems of Language in the History of Philosophy and Science 1626–1800* (Manchester UP, 1987) and of *The Companion to the History of Modern Western Science* (Routledge, 1989). He is working at present on a study of eighteenth-century natural history and on the Blackwell *Guide to Good Science Fiction* with Tom Shippey.

Robert Crossley, Professor of English at the University of Massachusetts at Boston, has written about a number of modern writers of science fiction and fantasy, including H. G. Wells, Olaf Stapledon, Octavia Butler, J. R. R. Tolkien, and Sylvia Townsend Warner. He has edited Stapledon's World War I correspondence and is currently writing the first full biography of Stapledon under a fellowship from the National Endowment for the Humanities.

Alan C. Elms is Professor of Psychology at the University of California, Davis. He is the author of

Personality in Politics (Harcourt Brace Jovanovich, 1976). He has written psychobiographical studies of Sigmund Freud, B. F. Skinner, Henry Kissinger, Alexander Haig, Vladimir Nabokov, and Jack Williamson. He is working on a full-length biography of Paul M. A. Linebarger (Cordwainer Smith).

John Huntington teaches English at the University of Illinois, Chicago. He is the author of *The Logic of Fantasy: H. G. Wells and Science Fiction* (Columbia UP, 1982), and of *Rationalizing Genius: Ideological Strategies in the American Science Fiction Short Story* (Rutgers UP, 1989).

Walter E. Meyers is Professor of English and Director of Composition at North Carolina State University. He has followed an interest in language through publications and studies ranging from medieval English literature to linguistics to science fiction. His *Aliens and Linguists* (University of Georgia Press, 1979) explores the connection between science fiction and linguistics in detail.

Tom Shippey is Professor of English Language and Medieval English Literature at the University of Leeds. He is the author of the *Road to Middle-earth* (Allen and Unwin, 1982), a study of Tolkien; and of several articles on such topics as 'cyberpunk', the Cold War in science fiction, and science fiction's images of history. He is preparing a collection of essays on ideology in science fiction, and working on the Blackwell *Guide to Good Science Fiction* with John Christie.

Alasdair Spark lectures in American history at King Alfred's College, Winchester. His particular interest is the Vietnam War, and he is the author of several articles on Vietnam subjects, most recently 'Flight Controls: the Social History of the Helicopter in Vietnam', in Jeff Walsh and Jim Aulich (eds), *Vietnam Images* (Macmillan, 1989). At present he is working on a second article on Vietnam and American science fiction, and completing his long-delayed doctoral dissertation on the morale of American soldiers during the Vietnam War.